The Author Blog: Easy Blogging for Busy Authors

Anne R. Allen

Published by Kotu Beach Press

ISBN: 978-1984090782

THE AUTHOR BLOG: EASY BLOGGING FOR BUSY AUTHORS: an easy-does-it guide to simple, low-tech blogging for authors who want to build a platform, but not let it take over their lives.

An author blog doesn't have to follow the rules that monetized business blogs do. This book teaches the secrets that made Anne R. Allen a multi-award-winning blogger and one of the top author-bloggers in the industry.

And you'll learn why having a successful author blog is easier than you think.

Here are some things you'll learn in this book:

- How an author blog is different — and easier to maintain — than a business blog
- What authors should blog about at different stages of their careers
- Choosing the right blog topics for your genre and audience
- How one type of blogpost can build your platform quickly
- Basic SEO tips that don't make your eyes glaze over with tech jargon
- How to write headers that will grab the attention of Web surfers
- How to keep your audience by learning the tricks of content writing
- Essential blog and social media etiquette rules
- What happens to your blog when you die?

Table of Contents

Kudos for Anne R. Allen's Blog...with Ruth Harris

"BRILLIANT! One of the Top 10 Resources for Self-Publishing Authors: Anne and Ruth's articles are humorous, enjoyable and informative." UK author Mark Tilbury.

"One of the most successful author-bloggers out there." Reedsy

One of "Ten Blogs and Websites Every Indie Author Should Know...Anne and frequent contributor Ruth Harris blog about a wide range of subjects pertinent to Indie authors." Big Al at Indies Unlimited.

"Want to work on your writing and your marketing? Then you've got to read Ruth Harris and Anne R. Allen's weekly blog. It's the best blend of rock-solid information mixed with an acerbic tone (at times) anywhere on the internet"...Frances Caballo at Social Media Just for Writers

"One of the 50 Kickass Resources for Indie Authors." Penny Sansevieri

"Is it any wonder why I love Anne R. Allen?" Publetariat

"One of the Top 15 Blogs for Indie Authors to Follow...I adore Anne's blog. Aside from being one smart lady, her mix of sass and education is priceless." Social media strategist and manager Frances Caballo

One of the "Blogs That Rock for Writers"...*Writer's Digest* editor Robert Lee Brewer

"I love following the blog of Anne R. Allen...for up-to-date tips and helpful articles for writers on what's current in the publishing world." Author D. G. Kaye.

"You know what a huge fan I am of Anne R. Allen's blog...absolutely marvelous." Romance author Collette Cameron

"Anne writes the essential blog for today's writers." Mystery author Carmen Amato.

"A must-read!" New Zealand author Maureen Crisp

"I recommend following the publishing blogs of both Jane Friedman and Anne R. Allen...I've implemented many of their tips, which have helped boost my SEO. *New York Times* bestseller Eileen Goudge in *Publisher's Weekly*

Foreword from Catherine Ryan Hyde

Although Anne wrote several chapters on author blogs in our writing guidebook, *How to be a Writer in the E-Age: a Self-Help Guide*, a number of our readers have asked for more information on blogging.

The popularity of the topic does not surprise me.

If you're a new author trying to get on your feet, or a more experienced author wanting to expand sales, the world is full of blogging and social media advice for you—much of it excruciatingly bad.

"Start a Twitter account and Tweet 'Buy my book!'" "Contact famous authors you've never met and ask them for blurbs!" "Send out newsletters using every email address you can get your hands on, whether their owners expressed interest in your newsletter or not!" "Start a blog and post chapters of your work-in-progress!"

Um… no. Don't. Any of the above, just don't.

One tool that's never a mistake is a well-done author's blog. But that's assuming you know how to do one well. And let's face it; no one is born knowing this stuff.

There isn't much blogging information out there aimed at authors rather than business bloggers, and you're not exactly a business. There's a level at which you are, but don't try to sell a book the way you'd sell a waffle iron. The rules for business blogging make the subject seem more complicated than it needs to be for the average author. You're blogging to sell books, not advertising, and the chances of turning off readers with an "ad approach" are all too real.

But no worries. Anne will straighten this out for you quite nicely.

Meanwhile I just want to go on record as saying that I do not have a newsletter. Authors swear by them, some publishers all but insist on them. I don't have one. What I do have is a blog with a simple method of subscription. Those wanting to follow my blog simply type in their email addresses and hit subscribe. That's it. Every time I add a new blog post, it's emailed to subscribers. I share publishing news—that's for me. I give away books and share deal alerts—that's for my readers. The one thing I never, ever do is send anything to any reader who did not ask to have it sent. In fact, when I post giveaways I ask readers to leave their email address and go on to promise "I will not use it for any purpose but to notify you if you win." I've never broken that promise.

Not too long ago I was part of a big "team giveaway." A bunch of authors got together to give away tons of books. At the end, the email addresses of everyone who entered were passed around to all the authors, so we could add them to our newsletter lists. I quietly deleted them. Then an odd thing happened. I started getting newsletters from the other authors. My email had been added to other peoples' lists. I couldn't unsubscribe fast enough!

How about you? How much do you love it when you express interest in a book or a shirt or a sofa and never stop hearing from the seller again?

This is what I love about blogs. When you write a new post you can blast the links on social media. Posts can be emailed to those who really are interested. But it's still information placed on the Internet, leaving readers to correctly feel that they are going out to access it, rather than having it forced down their throats.

In this modern world of Internet sales, there are many wrong ways to get attention. This is a right one.

And nobody knows more about blogging for authors than Anne. Better yet, her approach to teaching you is non-techy, easy to understand, and friendly. If you don't believe me, just keep reading.

Catherine Ryan Hyde

New York Times bestselling author of 32 published and forthcoming books

1—Author Blogging is Easier than You Think

"You need to blog!"

Authors hear that from everybody these days. Agents, publishers, and self-publishing gurus all advise authors to start blogging.

You cringe. The challenge can seem overwhelming — especially for creative writers.

How can you work on a novel or memoir if you're spending every day blogging?

The truth is you can't. And you shouldn't.

If you write fiction or memoir and think you have to blog every day, or even every week, you're reading the wrong blogging advice.

Here's the thing: most blogging advice is aimed at people who want to blog for its own sake. These are the bloggers who plan to sell advertising and monetize a blog as a business.

But as an author, you're blogging for name recognition and publicity for your books, which means most of the blogging "rules" don't apply to you. There are tons of blogging books and courses out there, but 80% of what they say has no relevance to you as an author.

Author blogs only need to appeal to your target book readership, not vast hordes of consumers. An author blog should be a fun, readable source of entertainment or information, not a hard-sell advertising machine.

An author blog only has to take a few hours a week — not the huge time commitment you've heard about. That's because when most people talk about blogging, they're only talking about *business* blogging — blogs that sell advertising.

But author blogs aren't about making money directly with ads. Instead they provide a platform for your writing and a way to communicate with readers and fellow writers.

The money will come later when you sell your books.

Are you giving your hard work away for free? Yes.

But think about how much hard work it takes to make the money to pay for the publicity, marketing and advertising required to make a book visible in today's marketplace.

Then a free author blog looks like a pretty good deal.

And it's easier than you think. Author bloggers don't need to build a huge audience. They only need a few engaged readers and can afford to build a readership slowly. (Blogging once a week or less is called "slow blogging" — which is fine for an author blog.)

Business blogs are all about numbers because the more hits they get, the more money they can draw from advertisers.

I don't mean to disrespect business bloggers. They work amazingly hard. I tried to monetize my blog once and it nearly killed me. Literally. I hardly had time to sleep or feed myself. I had to give up writing fiction entirely.

Business blogging requires knowledge of advertising strategies and the specialized art of copywriting. Business bloggers need to be able to pack a piece with keywords, know the best strategies for SEO (Search Engine Optimization) plus keep up with all of Google's ever-changing rules and algorithms.

Unfortunately, a lot of authors read "blogging" advice and take expensive "blogging" courses, and don't realize those are all about *business* blogging, not *author* blogging.

That puts authors through unnecessary stress.

Hey, we have enough stress already. We have to deal with endless rejections (yeah, they pretty much never stop) plus nasty reviews, difficult editors, evaporating agents, endless marketing, and a whole lot of other things those business bloggers don't have to worry about.

Author blogging is so different from business blogging that I wish it had a different name. Maybe we could call it "A-Blogging" as opposed to "B-Blogging."

The word "blog" is a newish invention anyway. It's a contraction of the term "Weblog," which was invented in 1997. The short form, "blog" was coined by a man named Peter Merholz, who whimsically broke the word "weblog" into the phrase " we blog" in the sidebar of his blog in 1999. "Blog" was first formally used as a verb a few months later by the legendary Evan Williams, founder of Blogger, Twitter and Medium.

The original blogs were personal diaries. It wasn't until the late 2000's that they became big business advertisers and newsmagazines.

Think of an author blog as being more like one of the original "weblogs."

I've written this book to help authors get back to that simple kind of blogging. I want to offer the basics of how to set up and maintain a simple author blog without a lot of complicated information and technology you don't need.

I started my blog knowing absolutely nothing about tech. I mean nothing. I'm a Boomer. I'm so old I remember when hand-held calculators were cutting edge technology. When I started my blog in 2009, I could send email, shop online, do a Google search, and that was about it.

But I figured out how to have a successful author blog without the help of even a resident teenager. In this book I'll tell you what I learned by trial and error.

Lots of error: I made the mistakes so you don't have to.

But mostly it's easy. As long as you ignore 80% of the blogging advice you read.

You don't need to advertise anything but you. You don't have to spend a penny. There are blog platforms that are absolutely free where you don't have to buy a domain name. And it doesn't have to take a big chunk out of your writing time.

I recommend authors blog once a week. When you're launching a blog, posting more often will jumpstart your search engine presence, so you might want to start out blogging more often, but you don't have to.

I do recommend posting your blog pieces on a regular timetable. You don't have to *write* to a timetable, but hit "publish" at generally the same day and time every week.

For years I tagged my blog with the message, "This blog is updated Sundays. Usually." After a while I could delete "usually." That kept the growing readership coming back every Sunday afternoon, knowing there would be new content.

This book is for authors—whether indie or traditionally-published—who want the platform blogging can provide, but don't want a blog to take over their lives.

2—How a Blog Helps an Author's Career

Does a blog sell books?

Not directly. Especially fiction.

It's also not a particularly good place to attract an agent (agents will glance at your blog if they're considering your query, but mostly to make sure you're not wearing a tinfoil hat.)

So what is blogging good for?

It's good for getting to know people and letting them get to know you. With a blog, you can meet people in the publishing industry as well as readers who will buy your books someday, even if you haven't written any yet.

The networking you do online is the key to establishing a writing career these days. I'm amazed at how many new writers still think a book launch is just something that happens at your local bookstore or a nearby book fair.

Today, a writer's market is global. Do you know the country where people read the most? India. Or where the second biggest population of English speakers lives? India. Followed by Pakistan and Nigeria.

So how can you get known by readers all over the planet? With your blog. You can reach more readers with one blogpost than with months of those painfully ill-attended "signings" or those $1000-a-pop book fair booths.

You don't have to go on an expensive blog tour, either. An informal series of guest posts and interviews with other writer-bloggers in your genre can get your book in front of just as many potential readers.

It certainly has worked for me. And I'm not the only author who's found blogging the key to career success. Listen to what author Nat Russo said after an expensive launch that failed to make any book sales.

"I slashed the number of book ads...and went back to blogging...sales rocketed...they leaped from 3/day to over 70/day, where they've remained ever since."

Got that? He stopped buying advertising and went back to blogging. That took him from a negative bottom line to making a nice living from his books.

Not only can blogging generate sales, it also gives you emotional support that you need as you're starting your career. Ours is a lonely profession. Connecting with people on the Web can give you moral support as well as information.

It also provides valuable contacts. You know how they always say you need to know somebody to break into publishing?

Blogging is a great way to get to know somebodies.

They don't have to be famous somebodies. Although who knows—maybe they'll be bigshots someday. Several of the bloggers I met early on became literary agents. Others write book reviews. Some are bestselling authors.

But most of all, blogging can reach readers.

John Green, superstar author of *The Fault in Our Stars* compared writing books to the kid's swimming pool tag game, "Marco Polo." He said that writing books is a life "in which you're in your basement alone for years and years, saying, 'Marco. Marco. Marco. Marco. Marco. And then if you're lucky, someone writes you and says ... Polo."

A blog provides people with a place to say "Polo."

I spent the first months of my blogging career saying "Marco", without getting many "Polos" in return, until I won a contest run by then Curtis Brown agent, Nathan Bransford.

The prize was a guest spot on his blog.

Then the Polos piled in. I started getting regular readers and making friends with them.

That's all "networking is" —making friends. And networking pays off.

How? Well, a year after I started my blog, I got offers from two publishers and an agent because they discovered me in the blogosphere.

Four years later, Ruth Harris, a *New York Times* million-selling author, joined the blog. We were getting 100,000 hits a month and made *Writers Digest's* list of the Best 101 Websites.

Guest bloggers included movie stars, Golden Globe winners, mega-sellers, literary agents, and even Nathan Bransford himself.

And as far as marketing, while other authors are desperately trying to get their books into bargain newsletters where they pay a huge amount of money to give some books away, I've had big, slick magazines, writer's conferences, and major websites come to me offering me free publicity for my books.

I've been interviewed for the fashion magazine *More* about "Fear of Homelessness in Older Women" (the subject of my mystery *No Place Like Home)* and for the *American Bar Association Journal* on "Amazon Customer Reviews" (which I satirize in *So Much for Buckingham.*) I've been invited to write for *Author* magazine on "How to Deal with the Time-Suck of Social Media," and I've been asked to write articles on writing craft for major magazines and books on the publishing industry, including *Writer's Digest* and *Writer's Market.*

Some of the books and magazines paid me a lot of money. Others gave me major publicity that would have cost me thousands of dollars.

Why did all this happen? Because I've blogged about subjects related to my books, and my blogposts come up on the first page of a Search Engine Results Page or "SERP." (I'll tell you the secret of why my posts get noticed later in the book).

All this happened because of a blog.

I'm not guaranteeing this will happen to you. And I'm not promising immediate results.

But a blog is the best way to build your brand and get your name out there so people have a chance of finding your book-needle in the vast bookselling haystack.

3—Blogging isn't "Over": 10 Reasons a Blog Helps your Career

If you tell your non-author friends you're thinking of starting a blog, at least one of them is bound to tell you that blogging is "totally over."

It's true that lots of people have been declaring blogging dead since at least 2012.

Google "blogging is dead" and you'll see thousands of entries.

Some people predicted blogging would die with the spread of the iPhone — but blogs got mobile-friendly.

Later people said blogging was dead when gossip-monger *Gawker* bit the dust — but blogs got classier.

Blogging turns out to be a pretty resilient medium that keeps changing with the times.

But your friends are right in one sense: the blogging-about-blogging blog is ready for the old folks' home.

That's because blogging about blogging is basically a pyramid scheme. You can only teach a finite number of people how to make money teaching blogging until the market gets saturated and everybody goes back to the current version of selling Amway.

But that stuff has nothing to do with author blogging, so smile sweetly and set your friends straight.

Here are ten of the best reasons I know for an author to blog. If you're a nonfiction author, the reasons are even more compelling.

All nonfiction authors need a platform, and a blog is the best way to build one.

Memoirists, especially, can start to gather an audience long before their book comes out. If they hope to publish a memoir traditionally, a blog following can be a big factor in whether a manuscript gets a read or not.

And even fiction writers need that online platform. You can't just have a launch party in your local bookstore and send a press release to your hometown newspaper and expect to make significant sales. (And even if you go the traditional publishing route, don't count on your publisher for much help with marketing.)

As I said, today's market is the entire planet. The advantage of a blog is that it can be your home in the global marketplace—a home where people can drop in and get to know you and find out about your books.

Whenever you query an agent or publisher or reviewer, or send a story to an anthology or literary magazine, the first thing people will do is Google you.

A blog is one of the best ways to make sure Google comes up with results that tell those people you're a professional author.

1) You Need a Website.

A blog is a website. Sending out a query when you don't have a website is usually a waste of time. Most agents and reviewers will reject on that item alone.

If you're getting lots of form rejections on a polished query, this may be the reason. Stop revising the query for the millionth time and start blogging.

All authors need to be Google-able these days. If you Google yourself and nothing comes up but a picture of you dressed as a leprechaun at that St. Patrick's Day bash in 2007, that's not going to impress agents, editors, reviewers or readers.

I know some excellent writers who never even get a nibble on their query letters and will spend thousands on writers' conferences and courses, but won't put in a few minutes a day on social media.

They say they won't bother with anything online because they're "serious" authors.

Well, they're probably going to remain serious, unpublished/unread authors unless they start doing something to get Google's attention.

Blogging is the easiest, fastest way to do that.

I'm not saying you should start blogging when you're a total newbie, or when you've just started that novel you've always wanted to write. Don't scatter your energies. If it's either blogging or writing the book, the book should always win.

But you'll need some kind of website when you're getting ready to send out queries or preparing to self-publish. So why not make it a blog?

2) A Blog Gets your Name into Google Faster than a Static Website.

A static website gets less traffic than an active blog, so the search engines won't notice it as quickly. The more active the site, the more likely the search engine spiders will find it.

A "spider" or" web crawler" is a software program that "crawls" through websites and reads information to create entries for a search engine index. Spiders will begin with a popular site, index the words on its pages and follow every link found within the site.

Search engines drive commerce these days. You need to be found. So those spiders are our friends.

A blog that's getting hits and comments will get noticed. Maybe not for a month or two, but it will get Google's attention. Then when somebody Googles you, you'll be on the first page of that all-important SERP.

Last year I experimented with a new once-a-week book

blog, and found it only took about four posts to get it on the first page of a search for "Anne R. Allen's Books."

So even a "slow blog" works pretty fast. It might take six months for a static website to get onto the first SERP, but a blog can get there in a matter of weeks.

3) Interacting with Readers

Author blogs are one of the best marketing tools out there, even if you don't have anything to market…yet.

As I said in Chapter #2, a blog is a fantastic place to make friends with people who may later buy your books. If you're blogging about the topic or setting of your novel or memoir, you will attract people who are familiar with the place or the situation you deal with in your book.

These connections are pure gold.

It's not that you want to try to hard-sell your book to everybody who wanders by. But these people can become contacts who can introduce you to corners of the Internet you might never have discovered otherwise. They can also end up introducing you to agents, editors, writers' conference directors, and other people who can make all the difference in your career.

Some blog contacts may buy your books and spread the word about them, some may be helpful with research, and a few may even turn into personal, long-time friends.

What's better than making friends? That is a great reason to blog right there!

4) You Already Know How to Write.

Blogging is writing. This is your medium. It's what you do.

So do it. It's a great way to polish your writing skills. And if you're a fiction writer, you'll learn to write better nonfiction, which you're going to have to do when you're marketing your books anyway.

You'll also get used to writing to a deadline. An important skill. And it's going to impress agents, editors and other bloggers that you're a serious writer who gets your work done on time.

5) Other Social Media Can Disappear.

Facebook has made it tougher for people to see your posts if you don't pay to boost them. And we don't want to forget MySpace or RedRoom...oh, whoops, I guess we already have.

Plus you might lose your account altogether. A few years ago, a lot of people found their Facebook accounts deleted because they used a "fake name" (even if the so-called fakery involved putting "Author" after their real name.)

That meant they had to start all over again getting friends and followers. It took months to get their following back — and some never did.

You can get kicked off any social media platform through no fault of your own. I got put in Facebook jail (shut out of my own page) for a week once because some troll falsely reported me as a spammer. And once Facebook slapped a CAPTCHA (one of those irritating "show-you're-not-a-robot thingies") on all my links for about six months for no reason I could see.

Now I'm not saying that "anything goes" in a blog, either. Bloggers have been kicked off Blogger for fine art that was deemed pornographic by some algorithm. Make sure you read the guidelines for the platform you choose.

6) Controlling your Brand

Every author needs to protect their "brand" — which is a jargon-y way of saying your name. "Stephen King" is a "brand." Ditto "Janet Evanovich" and "James Patterson." People buy the brand because they know what they're going to get.

Unfortunately, the Internet is infested with trolls, hackers, rage addicts, and spammers who can ruin your brand. I know a woman whose Facebook account got hacked by some diet-drug spammer who hit all her Facebook friends with insulting ads.

Several promptly "unfriended" her before she even knew

what happened. She got branded a hustler and fat-shamer.

Another friend got hit by a porn site who "tagged" a bunch of amateur porn with his name so it went all over his Facebook page.

This didn't do him any favors selling his children's books.

Unfortunately, stuff like this happens every day.

But on your own blog, you can defend yourself. There's that nice "delete" button. A troll, spammer or furious fool shows up and you click the button. All gone.

Social media comes and goes, but a blog is your own domain. You can kick out the troublemakers and make your own rules. If you want a politics-free zone, you can have it.

In these days of fake news and cyberbullying, you really want to have someplace online where you can interact with people and nobody will come barging in with fists flying, trying to pick a fight.

You can also create your own look and the atmosphere that will attract the kind of readers who are most likely to be interested in your work.

7) It Doesn't Have to Cost Anything.

Most book marketing is pretty pricey. But blogging doesn't have to cost you a thing.

Yes, you'll hear a lot of people saying you need an expensive, self-hosted blog and you should pay a designer to set it up for you, because OMG what will happen when you start getting ten million hits an hour and your blog crashes?

And others will echo Nate Hoffelder at The Digital Reader: "if you set up your business on either Blogger or WordPress . com, you could look like an amateur...would you really respect and trust a financial analyst whose site was yourmoney . wordpress . com?"

Here's the thing: you're not a financial analyst. Or a business blogger. You're a professional author, but not a professional *blogger*. And most book readers aren't techno-snobs. They don't respect or disrespect somebody based on their website's URL.

Sorry to pop anybody's bubble, but author blogs don't get millions of hits. They may get thousands, but that's not a problem. When our freebie blog was on Blogger, it got up to 5000 hits a day—which is a whole lot for a non-monetized blog—and it never crashed.

We moved from Blogger to a self-hosted site after the blog was hacked and pirated and I got locked out by the hacker. That is one possible hazard if you're getting 5000 hits a day. But that many hits are unlikely to show up on the average author blog.

Setting up a free WordPress dot com (non-self-hosted) blog is a little techier than setting up with Blogger, but most people can set one up their own.

You can also blog free on a number of sites like Goodreads and Medium, which are an option I'll explore in a later chapter.

And if you already have a website, adding a blog to it is a great option.

8) It Establishes You as a Professional

A blog is your online calling card. It's like your own international newspaper column. Writing to deadline and coming up with a topic once a week is great for building your writing muscles and impressing others with your professionalism.

Plus writing for a blog teaches you to write for the digital age.

By checking your stats, you can see immediately what posts are getting the most traffic and learn what works for a Web-based audience.

You'll also learn to use SEO (Search Engine Optimization) keywords, bulleting, sub-headers and white space to draw the eye through a post. This is useful for composing any kind of content for the Web.

When you have books to sell, you need to know how to

write guest blogposts (one of the best methods of marketing your book) as well as other Web content. Practicing on your own blog, even before you're published, gives you a big advantage.

9) Practicing is Good for Your Craft.

It's amazing how my writing improved — even my fiction writing — when I started blogging on a regular basis. Writing for an immediate audience is different from writing alone on your WIP (Work in Progress.) It gives you the boost of adrenaline that actors get when there's a real audience as opposed to acting in rehearsal.

That boost will take your writing to the next level. The more you do it, the better you'll get.

10) It Builds Platform.

Whether you're planning to self-publish or you're going the traditional route, every author needs a "platform" sooner or later.

Sooner is better.

When should you think about your platform?

Definitely as soon as you're ready to send out a story or submit a manuscript to an agent.

I know some authors obsess too much about platform and waste time on pointless overkill, but many writers ignore platform-building entirely, often because they're not quite clear on what it means.

It's true that "platform" isn't easy to define. Jane Friedman, former *Writer's Digest* editor, has written extensively about author platforms. Here's what she says agents mean when they say they're looking for author with platform:

"They're looking for someone with visibility and authority that has proven reach to a target audience."

This is especially true for nonfiction authors. But as I said earlier, no matter what you write, agents, editors, reviewers and fellow bloggers are going to search for you on Google.

The results are a good indication of your platform.

Self-publishers especially need to work on platform building. Many book marketers say authors should spend most of their social media marketing time working on platform rather than selling books directly.

Build that platform and the sales will come.

4—Why a Blog is Essential for Memoirists

I urge all nonfiction authors, especially memoirists, to start a blog as soon as possible.

The truth is that book-length memoir is tough to market. Especially if you're hoping for traditional publication.

That's because memoir is the toughest kind of book to write well. A book-length memoir needs to be crafted like a novel, with a story arc, compelling dialogue, and tight pacing. (Otherwise it's not memoir, it's autobiography.)

But real life doesn't have a story arc, compelling dialogue, and good pacing.

That means you have to superimpose those things on a story that already exists, instead of creating your story around a structure the way you do with a novel.

Recently, in an article called "Why Your Memoir Won't Sell", former *Writer's Digest* editor Jane Friedman listed things that will make an agent or publisher reject a memoir by somebody who isn't famous,

She says they'll probably turn it down if it is:

1) Your first book

2) Pain-focused

3) A collection of letters and other nostalgia pieces

4) An autobiography

5) A series of vignettes without a story arc

6) Somebody else's story

7) The writing isn't spectacular.

But none of those things are a problem on a blog. Most of what people read online is nonfiction, and readers love stories with heart.

Blogs are *made* for short personal essays. With illustrations. That means they are probably the most effective way to write your memoir. Later, you can make the blogposts into a book.

But do note that the book will need considerable editing. You don't want to cut and paste your blog word for word. Amazon now will remove a book that their robots say is "content that's freely available on the web."

And if you publish traditionally, you may be asked to take down the posts that end up in the book because of "non-compete" rules.

Also, a blogged short piece may not be eligible for contests or "first rights" publication in a traditional magazine, but that doesn't mean you can't do a different version of it, polish it up and repurpose it.

Desert Storm veteran Linda Maye Adams found a blog was the perfect venue for her to write about her war experiences. After years of trying to write about her service both as book-length memoir and as a novel, she finally found her voice in a blog.

Linda said: "The memoir came as a series of blog posts for the Desert Storm anniversary. They were focused on the question that had stymied me in the early days: "What was it like?" I used no people–it was all things like what I experienced when I deployed, what it was like when I got to Saudi Arabia, what it felt like when the war started. The blog format actually worked very well for me because it helped me compartmentalize the sections. As it turned out, there was a story there, but not the one that I would have told 25 years ago."

Even if you've finished your memoir, or are in the final stages of polishing, you can use segments of your book in blogposts and add lots of photos (expensive to put into books, but magnets for blog readers.)

For military memoirs, sharing photos of the place, people, and memorabilia can draw an audience of others who lived through the time as well as history and memorabilia buffs. When you publish the book, you'll have a ready-made audience.

Also, it's helpful to be aware that short, creative nonfiction is much more in demand than book-length memoir by non-celebrities.

You can market short pieces excerpted from your memoir while you're polishing up that book-length work. You'll be building platform and can even make some money. You can market short personal essays excerpted from your memoir to magazines, "Chicken Soup" type anthologies, journals, websites, and blogs.

And the easiest place to publish them is blogs — both your own and as a guest post on sites that address your issues or topics.

Plus if you can get an audience for your short personal "memoiric" essays, you'll have a much better shot at getting a publishing contract and/or readership for the full-length version.

5—Five Bad Reasons to Start an Author Blog

Okay, I've given you some good reasons to blog. But some people start blogs for the wrong reasons and get discouraged fast. Here are some of the bad reasons to start that blog.

1) To Get Rich Quick

Nothing infuriates me more than those books and blogs promising aspiring bloggers they can make a gazillion dollars of "passive income" with a blog in the next month if they take this overpriced course or buy that book of rehashed advice from 2005.

Don't plan for your blog to make money. An author blog is for building platform, not generating direct income.

Besides, the only people making "passive income" from blogging—even business blogging—are the people selling the overpriced courses and worthless advice. Blogging for "passive income" is basically a pyramid scheme. Pyramid schemes always provide "passive income" for the people at the top of the pyramid. That's not going to be you.

And the blogging about blogging pyramid has pretty much crumbled from old age at this point.

Blogging is work. Writing is work. There's nothing "passive" about it. Anybody who tells you otherwise is lying.

I used to subscribe to a couple of hype-y "how-to-blog" blogs, but I had to unsubscribe because these people are getting so desperate. One blog guru now sends an email fifteen minutes after you click through to read his post saying, "You've had enough time to read my post. Now share it to Facebook."

Creepy!! I'd just shared his post to Twitter, but I deleted the Tweet and unsubscribed. You're not the boss of me, dude.

Another sad truth is that Internet ads pay less than they used to. You're not going to make more than pennies a day from ads on a blog (especially "affiliate" ads that only pay when somebody clicks through and buys something.)

Since it's possible to have a blog that costs nothing, I think it's best to do no-overhead blogging and only monetize by advertising your own books. (And I don't recommend selling directly from your blog unless you've got a lot of tech skills and dozens of books. The logistics of using PayPal, credit cards, and keeping your site secure are complicated and expensive.)

Author blogs are for promoting your own brand. You're making money by not spending it on advertising elsewhere.

2) Overnight Fortune and Fame

Alas, the days of *Julie/Julia* are over.

When Julie Powell started her Julia Child blog in 2002, the term "blog" itself was only three years old. Blogging was a whole new concept.

Now, WordPress alone, with about a quarter of the market, hosts more than 76.5 million blogs. The odds for instant fame are not on your side. I highly recommend that authors blog, but we need to be patient.

3) Self-Examination

Journaling is a great aid to mental health. It can also get your creative juices flowing. I'm a firm believer in those "morning pages" Julia Cameron talks about in her iconic self-help book, *The Artist's Way.* Cameron describes them as "three pages of longhand, stream of consciousness writing, done first thing in the morning."

Whenever I'm going through a rough patch, I go back to

morning journaling and it always helps.

But you know what I don't do?

I don't publish the stuff. Because good journaling is by definition bad writing. It's dumping your unresolved issues on the page so you can examine them. You. Not anybody else.

Other people don't care. That's why shrinks charge the big bucks. The unresolved issues of strangers are amazingly boring.

And think what the trolls and fake news nuts could do with all that personal stuff about you if you do get famous.

This is why paper journals are still such a great boon to creatives. You might even want to get an old fashioned diary with a lock on it. Not much of our lives is private these days, so grab what little privacy you can still find.

Don't blog your angst. Think of your reader, not your own needs.

4) Dishing the Dirt

Blogging in order to dish the dirt on teachers, colleagues, exes, or even celebrities is likely to backfire unless you're brilliantly funny. (Or you're a clever Macedonian teenager who knows how to make money generating ridiculous disinformation on political candidates.)

Put that anger into your private journal (see above) and use it in fiction later.

5) Landing an Agent

There may have been a time, back in the early days of the millennium, when agents perused blogs looking for clients.

I don't think they ever looked to blogs for novels — because novels rely on good structure, and the structure of a blogpost shows nothing about your abilities to structure a novel.

But they may have gone looking for nonfiction.

However, that was the Jurassic period in terms of Internet history.

This is the age of the e-query. Agents get hundreds of

queries a day in their inboxes. They don't need to look elsewhere for amateur writing. The way to attract an agent is to write an outstanding professional query. If you've got a popular blog you think you can turn into a book, then put together a fantastic book proposal and a query that will knock their socks off.

But you shouldn't expect agents to wander by your blog with an offer of representation any more than you'd expect them to wander into your bedroom with a six figure advance.

Lots of blogs have been turned into bestselling books, and I think for nonfiction writers, starting your book as a blog is an excellent idea.

But don't expect an agent to come calling without some serious effort on your part.

***

These are not the right goals for an author-blogger, but there are plenty of good reasons for an author to blog, so read on!

6—Before You Start: How to Get an Online Profile

Even if you're not ready to start a blog yet, and you've never interacted with bloggers, you need to start by getting an online profile. This will allow you to comment on blogs, which is the first step in blogging (see chapter #7.)

You need three things before you sign up.

1) A Consistent Professional Author Name.

I'm not telling you to use a pen name, which can make things more difficult than they need to be. (See chapter #27, "Should you Use a Pen Name?")

But be mindful when you choose how you're going to present your name as an author.

How will it look on a book cover? If it's very long, you might want to use some initials.

How many other people are using it? My first two books were published under the name "Anne Allen" and if you Googled me, you could not find me or my books. My name is one of the most common women's names in the English-speaking world. There are five of us in my small-town doctor's practice alone.

So Google your name before you make the final decision. (Put your name in "quotes" for a more accurate search.) This will tell you if somebody is out there making a name for herself that happens to be the same as yours.

To stand out, I added my middle initial. Everywhere I go

on the Web, I'm annerallen. There are other Anne R. Allens out there, but not as many, and at the moment Google gives me top billing.

Making your name unique is especially important if you share it with somebody famous. So if your real name is Kim Kardashian or Justin Bieber, choose a pseudonym or trot out a middle name, initial, or use a nickname. Try K. C. Kardashian or J. Montague Bieber.

You want to make this decision before you start to set up your profiles, or you're going to be adding to the other Justin Bieber's platform, not building your own.

And don't use a cutsie moniker. Unless you plan to write all your books under the *nom de plume* "ScribblerSally" or "randomthoughts," you don't want to comment on blogs with that handle.

Always use your professional name online, because you're building a professional platform.

2) Author Bio.

I have a whole chapter (#13) on how to write different kinds of author bios. What you want here is about three paragraphs of the most important things you want agents, readers, and colleagues to know about you.

Make sure you put "writer" in your "employment" even if you're not getting paid to write yet. If you tag yourself as a writer, that will come up in a Google search.

3) Author Photo.

The best kind of photo is a friendly, smiling head shot of yourself in tight close-up. If you don't have an author photo, you might be able to crop an existing photo, or even use a selfie, as long as it's professional and friendly looking.

Do use a picture of yourself. Your adult self.

Not you and your hubby in fond embrace. Not your cat or a baby picture. It needs to be a grown-up, professional-looking picture of you. With clothes on. Beachy photos end up looking like porn spam in thumbnails. Even if you write erotica, save the skin for your website.

Again—be professional. This is all about creating an image of yourself as trustworthy, intelligent, and reliable.

Three Easy Ways to Get an Online Profile

1) A Gmail Account

If you have a gmail account, you have a Google ID. It's not as useful as the old Google Plus ID, but it will open blog doors.

2) A Gravatar ID.

Gravatar is a universally recognized image ("avatar") that follows you from site to site appearing beside your name when you comment or post on a blog. You can register an account using your email address. Your photo should be square—up to 2000 pixels.

This gives you an image ID that will work on pretty much every blog to sign in to comment. Clicking on your image on that blog will lead people to your Gravatar ID, where you can put links to your sites. When people read a comment, they can click on your image and find you on the Web.

2) Join WordPress with a "Username" Account

It's possible to join the WordPress blogging platform without having a WordPress blog. You can sign up for a "username only account."

Unfortunately, Blogger, which is owned by Google, sometimes doesn't accept a WordPress ID, so a Google ID is better for a Blogger (blogspot . com) blog. Tech companies always seem to be at war with each other and they don't seem to mind the collateral damage.

The important thing is to take the few minutes to sign up for one of these IDs, so you can comment on blogs without jumping through hoops, and clicking on your name or picture will allow people to find you.

7—Commenting on Blogs: The First Step to Blogging Success

I know the prospect of building an online platform can feel daunting to a lot of new writers, especially those of us who didn't grow up with tech. I've heard all the moans and wails:

- "But I'm still working on my first novel."
- "I don't have time for that social media nonsense. Nobody cares what I had for lunch!"
- "I'm a serious literary writer. I'm not going to waste time on childish things."
- "I'm not going to take up blogging at my age."
- "I'm already on Facebook. Isn't that enough?"

But there's something quick, easy and relatively painless you can do right now to raise your search engine profile that won't take more than a couple of minutes from your writing time.

Ready for it?

Ta-da!

Comment on blogs!

It's a powerful tool.

Commenting on other blogs is the step most new bloggers skip. They want to sit in their own little blogs waiting for readers like a spider with a web.

But blogging is a social medium, and you need to go out and socialize.

Interacting on blogs is a great way to make friends. And in the end, that's what a platform really is: how many people feel they "know" you well enough to want to buy one of your books.

A comment on our blog can put your name in front of 30,000+ people in a week. It could take years to reach that many people with a brand new blog.

Commenting on high profile blogs is the quickest way to get into search engines. Most of my early mentions on Google came from my comments on other people's blogs.

In fact, my blog took off because of a guest post on another writer's blog, not my own. That's how people learned my name and style (more on this in Chapter #23 on guest blogging.)

Discussions on high-profile blogs can lead to discussions on your own. Find yourself making a long comment? That's your next blogpost! Invite people to discuss it further on your own blog.

Support somebody's argument on a high-profile blog and you have a blog friend. That's how I got my first followers.

Comments on well-known blogs that are on Google's radar will get your name onto that search page. (Comments on more obscure blogs that have been set up by somebody schooled in SEO can be good, too.)

I'm not just talking about writing blogs like mine.

A comment on any blog that interests you—and your potential readership—will work.

I know writers new to the world of social media and blogging have lots of reasons for not commenting. I hear them a lot.

1) "But I can't even find the comments!"

A lot of older writers find the whole concept of blogging weird and unfathomable. I remember being frustrated when I first started.

Sometimes I'd find comments, and sometimes I wouldn't.

Sometimes I'd land on one post with a thread of comments after it, but sometimes I'd get a whole string of posts with nothing but a thingy at the end saying "37 comments".

Here's the little trick "everybody knows" so they don't bother to tell you —

Click on the "37 comments" (or whatever number) and that will open the post in a new page where all the comments appear at the end of the post. Some blog formats make you hunt around in the sidebar for the "comments" link, but it's there. Keep looking.

Some blogs, like ours, will allow you to reply to a particular comment if you hit the "reply" button under that comment.

Or you can leave a general comment if you hit "Leave a Comment" at the bottom of the whole thread. (On some WordPress blogs the comment button is at the top of the thread.)

If you want to go back to the home page that lists all the recent blog posts, without comments, click on the header (title of the blog) or the word "blog", or the link to the "home" page.

See? It's not so hard when somebody tells you what to look for.

2) "I don't want to comment on your blog — or Kristen Lamb's or Jami Gold's — because you guys never comment on mine."

Popular blogger Jami Gold has run into this as much as I have. This is how she responded: "Some commenters feel that high profile bloggers are obligated to comment on the blogs of everybody who leaves a comment. I've certainly heard from a number of them. They sometimes even leave a comment saying 'I'm commenting here, so now you need to visit my blog and comment'."

This may come from a simple kindergarten sense of "fairness," but Jami thinks it also may come from a misunderstanding of the kind of advice I'm giving here.

So please! Don't think I'm saying you should comment on big blogs to get the blogger to reciprocate on yours.

That's not the reason to do it. You're writing a comment to get the attention of search engines and blog readers.

Commenting on a big name blog puts you on Google's radar. The digital spiders that crawl around the web already know the big, high profile blogs. If you're on a high profile blog, the spiders will pick up your name. If somebody Googles you, that comment will come up.

Also, commenting on blogs is great for networking. If somebody likes your comment, they may look you up and maybe even buy your book.

A comment may also get the attention of the host blogger, which is a good thing, not so they'll comment on your blog, but maybe you'll be invited to guest post, or they might mention you in a future post.

However, there can't be a *quid pro quo* for all comments, even though that might seem "unfair." This is because nobody can read and comment on 10,000 blogs a day.

I do stop by the blogs of our regular visitors when I have time. I don't always comment, but I do try to keep track. However, readers need to remember we're all in the business of writing books, and the old WIP has to come first.

The important thing to remember is that the blogger doesn't benefit that much from one more comment, but if you're a newbie trying to build platform, that comment is a big plus for *you*.

3) "I prefer to send the blogger a DM or email."

Sure. That's fine. Sometimes the blogger will have time to give you a personal answer. I try to answer all our readers' emails, even though it's time-consuming and I sometimes confront so many emails in the morning that I just want to go back to bed and hide.

But my e-mailed answer is no more personal than my answer in a comment thread, and nobody will see it but you and me.

Every week, people send me personal emails saying they liked a post from me or Ruth or one of our guests, and of course we appreciate it. We always like to hear that people are benefiting from our posts.

But many writers mention their own books and pitch them to me.

So let's stop a minute and think about this: what's better for you, the author?

1) Getting your book title in front of me, the world's slowest reader, who has over 500 unread books in my TBR list?

2) Getting your book title in front of the thousands of people who read our blog?

Are you seeing why it's better to put your feedback (and name) into a comment?

Plus, if you have a question, you can be pretty sure other readers have it too. If I answer in the comments, rather than in a personal email, that's helping all our readers, not just you.

4) "I can't figure out how to write a comment."

Okay: this is a biggie. New tech can be daunting. Nobody likes to be rejected, especially by some stupid machine.

But you just signed up for that online ID, remember? So you're golden. When that window comes up that asks for your ID, put that in. If they don't take it, use another. Gravatar and Google should open any blog comment door.

5) "I have no idea what to say."

I understand. Writers are shy persons. We'd rather lurk in the shadows. I lurked for about a year before I started commenting on blogs. Nothing wrong with it. Do lurk for a while if you're just starting in the blogosphere.

But eventually you'll probably feel moved to say something.

Most bloggers will put some questions at the bottom of the post to invite comments. Good questions will invite you to share your own opinions or experiences with the topic.

Read the comments. You may want to respond to one of them. That's a good place to start.

You don't have to heap praise on the blogger. Bloggers like praise as much as anybody, but it's best to say something that adds to the discussion. That doesn't mean you should be confrontational or put the blogger down, either. (That's a good way to get deleted.) But say something like, "Love these 3 tips for getting your cat to eat dry food, and I'd like to add#4..."

Or you can say, "I understand what you're saying about only blogging nonfiction ...but I blog daily cat haikus, and I have 400 followers who love them." You can even include a link to the blog. One link is usually acceptable in a blog comment.

Every rule has an exception and if you're it, let people know.

You can even say something like, "I'm glad you say it's okay to be a slow writer. It took me ten years to write *Love is a Cat from Hell,* but I finally launched it last week."

Don't put in a link to your retail buy page—that can get you blocked for spam—but a mention of your book and a link to your blog is fine.

Or start a discussion with other commenters with something like, "I love what ScribblerSally said about Maine Coon cats in her comment."

This can bring the added perk that ScribblerSally might click on your name to find out more about you and your cat. If you've joined Gravatar, that will take her to a profile with an address for your blog and an email address.

Then Sally may follow your blog or even buy your book.

You can also say, "I've quoted this post on my blog today and we're having a lively discussion."

The most useful comments add something to your "authority." So if you can say stuff like "I was in law enforcement for twenty years and this is what really happens when somebody reports a missing cat..." Or "I'm a health practitioner who also writes cat haiku and I have proof that cat poetry has healing properties."

An added perk comes when that little fragment of text comes up in the Google search of your name. It will show your name and "I was in law enforcement for 20 years..." or "I'm a health practitioner..."

This is a huge help to agents, reviewers, and other people who are trying to find out if you're a reliable person they want to work with.

Guidelines for Blog Comments

A good blog comment can be anything from 10 to 300 words. If you feel the need to go longer, you probably have a blogpost of your own there. (Write it down and save it!)

Other than that, almost anything goes in a blog comment, with a few caveats:

1) Skip the spam.

Don't talk up your book or blog in a comment unless it's relevant to the conversation. That's considered spamming:

- "I respect your opinion on prologues, but I've got testimonials from readers who love prologues—the longer the better—over at my blog today" is great.
- "This discussion of Marcel Proust reminds me of my book, *Fangs for the Memories,* a zombipocolyptic vampire erotic romance, $3.99 on Smashwords." Not so much.

Ditto links to your website or buy pages if they don't illustrate a relevant point. Begging people to read your blog is spammy, too. If you have more than one link in a post, spambots will often dump you directly into spam, so your comment will be in vain anyway.

2) Don't act like a troll.

Saying insulting things about the blogger or other commenters, or using language that's inappropriate will get you deleted. Ditto political diatribes or religious screeds. Be professional and polite.

3) Read the whole post.

I get so many comments from people who have only read the first line of a post, that I wonder if half the people online are reading-impaired. It only makes you look like a doofus when you tell the blogger, "you should have said this, that and the other thing" ...when they said exactly those things in the second paragraph.

4) Read other comments.

Sometimes there are 100s, so you'll probably only be able to skim them, but do be aware of what other people are saying so you don't repeat what somebody else has said. Comments are meant for discussion, so remember you're talking to everybody who's reading and commenting, not just the host blogger.

5) No emotional blackmail.

Don't say, "I just followed this blog, so now you have to follow my five blogs, like my Facebook page, follow me on Twitter and get me a double decaf latte while you pick up my dry cleaning." If you demand any kind of *quid pro quo* for a comment or a follow, you'll look like a jerk to the whole community.

6) Don't whine or throw shade.

Dissing Amazon, agents, the publishing business, or trash-talking a bestselling author will not work in your favor. Ditto complaining about how nobody reads your blog.

Getting your blog noticed by search engines involves many factors: SEO, tech savvy, Tweetable headlines, and original, general-interest content.

Nobody owes you readership.

Besides, every author does not need a high profile blog. You simply need a place where fans can find you. High profile blogs have their disadvantages. Like hackers might hijack your content and lock you out of your own blog. Not a fun experience.

And your inbox will be jammed with pitches from wannabe guest bloggers who want to use your blog to sell sunglasses or porn and who are too lazy to visit a blog and find out what it's about before they query. (Grrr.)

7) Don't expect high profile bloggers to follow you back or critique your blog.

This isn't because they're snotty. But as I mentioned above, even bloggers only have twenty-four hours in our days. We have to spend some of those hours writing stuff that pays.

8) Don't promote your blog with @ messages to individuals.

When sharing your new blogpost on social media, don't send it to individuals via @ message on Twitter. Especially people you don't follow. It's considered really rude to send advertising via @message. It will get you blocked and unfollowed.

How to Find Blogs Where a Comment will get Exposure

To find the big blogs in the publishing industry, just go around to a few writers' blogs. Many will have a "blogroll" in the sidebar.

We don't have a blogroll, but we have a "resources" page. There you'll find links to blogs I recommend. But don't feel you have to read them all. Subscribe to a handful and drop in on others when you see them mentioned elsewhere. Reading blogs can become a time-suck, and writing your WIP has to be your #1 priority, always.

1) Do they have a lot of followers?

Not all blogs list the number of followers they have, but some do.

Blogs that have more than 500 followers have probably been around a while, so the search engines will have found them.

2) What about comments?

Blogs with a lot of comments are probably being read by

many people, since generally less than 2% of readers comment.

However, some top blogs don't get any comments at all. Joel Friedlander's and Jane Friedman's usually don't get more than a handful, but they're a great place for Google to find you.

3) Check with Alexa.

Not the one on your Amazon devices. This Alexa is a worldwide website ranking system. Just copy the URL (web address) for any website and paste it in their search window labeled "Browse Top Sites." You don't have to be a paid subscriber to get the basic data on a site.

As of this writing, Alexa lists the top 10 websites in the world as #1 Google, #2 You Tube, #3 Facebook, #4 Baidu (the Chinese language search engine) #5 Wikipedia, #6 Yahoo, #7 Google India, #8 Reddit, #9 Qq (another Chinese site), #10 Taobao . com (The Chinese Amazon)

A blog with an Alexa rating of 900K or less is getting a whole lot of readers, since there are billions of websites. (Alexa measures all websites, not just blogs.) So commenting on a blog with a low Alexa rate will raise your profile.

Commenting on Smaller Blogs is Good, Too.

Don't just comment on the biggest blogs. Comment on the blogs that interest you—your favorite author's blog, cat blogs, food blogs.

(But avoid the snark-infested waters of political blogs unless you're a political writer or using a pseudonym.)

Alexa ratings rise and fall, but your comment is forever. It may be picked up years from now by some search engine that hasn't even been invented yet. And be aware that a smaller, niche blog with an engaged audience can be much more useful to you in the long run. If that niche happens to be your target demographic, you'll reach the people who are most likely to buy your book.

8—When Should an Author Start a Blog?

This depends on what you write. As I said earlier, if you write nonfiction, especially memoir, how-to or self-help, you want to start much earlier than if you write fiction.

I don't agree with the people who pressure every newbie writer to fritter away precious writing time on social media. Don't get me wrong: in order to be a marketable writer, you do need a blog or website. It's how you establish your brand. But until you've been writing for a while, you may not have a clue what that brand is going to be.

What if zombies invade the second draft of what started out as a cozy mystery? Or a Victorian romance veers into steampunk? What if romance writer Rosa Lee Hawkins decides to become dark, brooding R. L. Hawk? Now she's stuck with that pink, lacy blog—plus the betrayal her romance-loving followers will feel.

You don't need a marketing tool until you've got something to market.

If you write fiction, don't worry about a blog until you've finished the rough draft of a novel and/or had a couple of stories published.

Nonfiction Writers

If you write primarily nonfiction—as a freelance essayist, journalist, or nonfiction book author—a blog is *essential* unless you are already a well-known authority in your field.

A blog is the fastest way to build audience and authority.

I know there are some freelancers who will say, "Why should I give away my work free on a blog? I'm a pro. I deserve to get paid." But times have changed. In the digital era, we have to use some of our writing as a way to network and sell our "brand."

As social media guru Dakota Shane says: "Instead of thinking of writing as your final product or offering, begin thinking about it as a MEANS TO AN END. Think of your writing as a way to showcase your expertise in a specific area." He points out that while blogging can't provide a source of income for most writers, it leads to other "revenue streams" like book sales, speaking engagements, consulting, and many more freelance gigs.

Freelance journalists should probably start a blog as soon as you hang out your shingle as a freelancer. Your blog is your portfolio on the Web: the place where people can stop by and see what you do as well as get to know you.

To establish yourself as an authority on a subject, you need your name to show up on that first page of a Google search.

The best way to get you on that SERP is by guest posting on major high-traffic blogs on that subject. I'll be talking more about that in the chapter on guest blogging.

For nonfiction writers, getting good guest blog gigs should be your number one goal.

And the way to learn to be a good blogger is to have your own blog. So start one as soon as you can and blog at least once a week on a regular schedule.

Fiction Writers

If you're pretty sure fiction is your primary medium, you don't have to rush into blogging. Some fiction writers start to blog too early in their careers and find it's a time-suck that keeps them from their writing goals.

For one thing, fiction itself doesn't usually work well on blogs. People are generally looking to skim a blogpost for information, not settle in for a cozy read. Serializing a novel on a blog generally usually doesn't draw much of a readership. (The best place to do that is on a site dedicated to serialized fiction, like Wattpad.)

Also a novel that's been blogged is considered "previously published" by most agents and publishers, so you're losing a lot of future opportunities. (More on this in Chapter #12, "What Not to Blog About.")

I'm not sure why, but even short fiction doesn't do that well on blogs. I know a big name author who tried to give away some short fiction on her blog and got only a handful of hits.

But she put the same stories as individual ebooks on Amazon, charged $2.99 each, and they were bestsellers. People would rather pay for a story in a bookstore than read it free on a blog, where it doesn't have a cover or proper book formatting.

This means a fiction writer needs to write nonfiction on a blog. (For ideas for what kind of nonfiction does well on a blog, see Chapter #11: "What Should an Author Blog About.")

That's one of the reasons why I don't think fiction writers have to worry about blogging if you're at a stage where you need to put 100% of your writing time into learning your craft and getting that first book out of your head and onto the page.

That's not to say there isn't a benefit from blogging early on. For some of us, blogging is just plain fun. Playing around with words is good at any stage of your writing career, as long as it doesn't keep you from your primary writing goals.

But blogging is a commitment. Don't start if you don't have the time or discipline to follow through. There's nothing sadder than an abandoned blog hanging out there in cyberspace attracting trolls, porn spam, and real estate ads from Mumbai.

People will Google you, come upon a blog that hasn't been updated for three years, and think you died.

Or worse, an abandoned blog can be hijacked by scammers who will use it to install malware on the computers of people who try to find you. This has happened to a number of my online friends. It's very common.

***

You definitely want to have a blog going by the time you start to send out queries or self-publish your first book. Remember that as an author, you're blogging to make yourself an interactive home on the Web—a place for agents, fellow writers, fellow bloggers, publishers, editors, and readers to find you and communicate with you.

So start when you're ready to communicate with them.

9—Medium: A Place to Get Your Blogging Feet Wet

Whether you write fiction or nonfiction, most successful blogposts are nonfiction, so if you're a novelist, learning to blog can be a steep learning curve. And as I've said, writing for blogs is a little different from writing magazine articles or creative nonfiction essays for anthologies.

One way to get your feet wet before you plunge into regular blogging is to post some pieces on the new(ish) blog platform, Medium.

Medium is a no-frills blogging platform where anybody can post. It was founded in 2012 by Evan Williams, the tech pioneer who also created Blogger and Twitter.

Williams' goal was to create a forum where it would be easy for people who have "thoughtful things to say," to share ideas. As of mid-2017, it had 60 million users. The writers represent all skill levels and all levels of society, from a high school kid discussing his identity crisis to President Obama urging citizens to vote.

What makes Medium different from other blogging platforms is that articles are grouped by topic rather than by author. So you don't have your own blog. You have a series of articles that will be grouped by whatever topic you "tag" them with.

That means you might post about writing on one day and your work will appear with other writing articles. But if the next day you write about how to teach your cat to use the toilet, you'll be grouped with the pet care articles.

A lot of writers use Medium to repost articles they have published somewhere else first, to reach a wider audience

But it's not the best platform to use as your main blogging venue. You can't interact with readers and you don't have your own page. Also, Medium is a bit precarious, and may not be sustainable in its current form.

It has had its share of growing pains. In January 2017, Mr. Williams fired a lot of staff when it became clear Medium wasn't making any money.

Later in the year, they rolled out a paid membership plan. There's now a two-tier system for readers. Authors can put what they consider their best work behind a paywall so the work will only be available to paid members (The fee for membership is $5 a month.) Non-paying readers are allowed three pieces of "premium" content per month.

The theory is that money generated from the membership will pay the authors of the "membership only" pieces.

A few months after they rolled out the membership option, Medium established the "clap" function to posts. Paid posts are recompensed according to the number of "claps" a post receives, and readers can clap as many times as they want.

Claps on a non-premium post don't result in payment, but they tell the author how popular the post is. Or they're supposed to. According to some writers, claps mostly tell how much time your reader has on his hands to hit the clap icon over and over. A lot of people think it's kind of silly. But as of this writing, the "clap" system seems to be here to stay.

I wouldn't recommend that a new blogger put your work behind the paywall, because you're going to be on Medium to reach readers, not make money. (And from what I hear, the paywall plan hasn't been well-received.)

There are hundreds of "publications" under the Medium umbrella, like *The Writing Cooperative, Cuepoint, The Coffeelicious, The Mission, Start-up Grind, Poets Unlimited*, etc. Also big publications like the *Washington Post* and *The Economist* have versions on Medium. Some publications like *The Awl* started on Medium and then spun off on their own.

Getting your work considered by one of those vetted publications is like submitting to any magazine. Each has its own editors and editorial policies. Some are much harder to break into than others. I've read that *Coffeelicious* gets about 50 submissions a day. Others get even more.

But you don't need to get into a publication to write on Medium. Anybody can post there, and signing up is easy, even for a less than tech-savvy author.

As I said, I don't recommend using Medium as your main blogging platform. But it's a good way to learn your blogging chops, get your name known, and maybe acquire some followers. It's also a good place to promote your own blog once you've started it. You can re-blog your most recent post, or even some "evergreen" (not dated) content, to reach a different audience. Author-Publisher Bob Mayer often re-blogs his posts of general interest on Medium after they have appeared on his blog.

But do be aware some people in the industry are predicting Medium's demise. Because it hasn't yet found a way to turn a profit, it may fade or disappear altogether, so make sure you save all your posts and don't count on the platform being available forever.

10—Essential Tips for Starting Your Author Blog

Here are some tips I learned along the way that can make blogging easier and more successful for authors. Some of these are the opposite of what you'll hear from the business blogging gurus.

But remember an author blog isn't the same as a business blog.

1) Put Your Name on it!

The most important thing for author-bloggers to remember when starting a blog is to *put your name on it.* The number one reason for an author to use social media is to get name recognition, so use your own name (or author pen name) in your title.

Anonymous blogging is wasted blogging.

You want people to be able to put your name into a search engine and find you. Don't make them rummage in their memory banks trying to remember if your blog is called "Songs from the Zombiepocalypse" or "Lost Marbles" or "Messages from Your Raccoon Overlords." Don't use a cute name the way business bloggers do.

That's because your product is *you.*

2) Write Enticing Headers.

How to write good headers is the #1 most important lesson for new bloggers to learn. Weak headers are probably the biggest cause of blog failures.

A blogpost title or "header" has to ask a question or offer a solution. It needs to grab people from an endless parade of Tweets and shares to say, "Pick me!"

I often find a blogpost I want to share, but the header says nothing, so I have to make one up, and often I don't have time.

So make it easier for people to Tweet and share your content. Don't use one-word titles. Tell people what's inside. Give as much information as possible to pique a reader's interest while keeping to an optimum length of around 70 characters.

A header is not the place to be a poet. Think like a copywriter instead. You want stuff like how-to's, lists, and questions. Think magazine cover teasers: stuff like "What Your Teacher Won't Tell You About the Oxford Comma!" Or "Does Chocolate Make You a Better Writer?"

Look at what you click on when you're skimming the web. Are you going to click through to read something titled "Meandering" or "Thoughts"?

Other people probably won't either.

3) Avoid the Thesaurus.

Another way to "optimize" those search engines is avoid getting thesaurus-happy. That means avoid using what grammarian H. W. Fowler called "elegant variation."

• Normal sentence: "It was a good bull, a strong bull, a bull bred to fight to the death."

• Elegant variation: "It was a good bull, a strong animal, a male creature of the bovine persuasion bred to do battle..."

Search engines that are looking for something about bulls will be drawn to that repetition you're trying to avoid. So go ahead and repeat yourself. (But not so much that you look like you're gaming the algorithms. Too many repeat words will be penalized with less visibility by SEO engines because they look like spam.)

4) Don't Try to Maintain a Lot of Blogs.

Do as I say and not what I do. I started a second blog

when the big blog got hijacked. When we got the blog back and moved it to a safer host, I used the new one as an experiment for this book.

But don't do this at home, kids. Dealing with two blogs put my new novel about eight months behind schedule.

If you write in very different genres under different names, you may need two blogs, but consider giving one of your personas a simple static website.

The Internet is littered with abandoned blogs. Unfortunately, the old ones show up higher in the search engines than a new one. So if you want make major changes with your blogging, you still want to continue to use the old URL, or at least leave a forwarding address on the old one.

If an agent or reader Googles you and finds a blog that hasn't been updated for years, they won't think much of your professionalism.

And unless you're a nun who writes erotica or somebody else who needs to keep your identity a secret, be wary of having a "personal" blog and a "professional" one. Nothing is secret in social media and everything you do online should be professional. (If you want to be online and private, I advise a "closed group" family Facebook page for personal family photos and news.)

And don't start another blog whenever you want to write on a different subject. That just scatters your audience and can drive you batty.

Most blogs have lots of pages. Use one page for fiction and one for nonfiction and another for stories about your pet gerbil. If you start out with a fantasy blog and decide to write historical romance instead, you can change everything: header, theme, photos.

Just keep the URL, because Google will always bring up the oldest website first.

5) Don't Forget "Share" Buttons.
Those are the little "f" "t" , "g+" and other buttons that

allow people to share your brilliant words to their Facebook, Twitter, Google+, Pinterest, etc. accounts. They are the way you will build a following.

Even if you don't use all those social media platforms, you want people who do to spread the word there.

It's frustrating to find a great post and want to share it and find no share button.

If possible, try to use buttons that include your Twitter handle (@yourname) so you'll get notifications when somebody Tweets your post.

6) Write a Welcoming "About Me" Page.

There's more about writing a bio in Chapter #13: "How to Write an Author Bio." Do you have any awards, publications, etc.? Have a claim to fame outside of writing—like winning the state fair pie cook-off or raising exotic gerbils? Have any online publications you can link to? This is where you crow about it. Especially if it's entertaining or amusing.

7) Invite Comments.

Ask a question at the end of the post—a call to action. This doesn't mean whining about how you need comments. Think of questions that relate to the reader. Ask them to talk about themselves.

If you've written a how-to blog about building birdhouses, ask them: "What about you—did you have as much trouble as I did building your first birdhouse? What craft project did you find the most daunting when you were a kid?"

Also, I think it's best not to moderate comments on your most recent post, unless you've got a real spam problem.

I prefer to moderate only comments of posts older than a week, since older posts attract the most spam.

8) Remember the "Social" in Social Media.

That means you have to reply to those comments, too!

Full disclosure: I didn't do that for an entire year. I was totally clueless.

Oh, yeah, and visit your followers' blogs as often as you can when you're starting out. Ruth and I don't have time to visit all 10,000+ of our readers these days, but I drop in on commenter's blogs from time to time. I always learn something.

9) Write for the Web Reader.

People skim on the Web. Don't post big hunks of text. White space is your friend. So are numbered lists, bullet points, bolding, etc. Anything over 2500 words is usually off-putting. More on this in chapter #15 on "How to Write Blog Content."

Posts should be at least 300 words long or Google will ignore them. People hate to be lured to a site only to find something super-short.

10) Use Sub-headers and Keywords.

Make sure you format sub-headers using the formatting tool in your toolbar. They make your text easier to read, plus the formatting makes the sub-headers into the "live" links those search engine spiders pick up on.

Use a sub-header for at least every 300 words of text.

You want at least one of your sub-headers to use your main keyword.

What are keywords? They're the words that most effectively let the public (and the search engines) know what your post is about. A "keyword" can be a phrase as well as a one-word topic. Always put your keyword in your title, plus at least one sub-header, and sprinkle them liberally through the post.

11) Choose Useful Images and Make Your Blog Easy to Read.

Images are essential for blogs these days, in a way that they were not when I started out.

When I started blogging in 2009, my old blog header photo that went out with all the posts was just fine.

Later, the "book of the week" became the featured image.

But that was in the days before Twitter images, Pinterest, and the rise of image importance on other social media. These days a blogpost without a sizable, recognizable image is pretty much invisible.

According to social media guru Frances Caballo, colored visuals increased people's willingness to read a piece of content by 80%. Content with relevant images gets 94% more views than content without relevant images.

If you're a photographer, you're golden here. You can simply upload your own images to illustrate your post.

But if you are using other people's images, be careful not to use anything that's copyrighted. Some bloggers do a quick Google search and use an image without making sure it's free to use.

Not a good idea. Six months later they may get a nasty surprise bill from the copyright holder. I know several bloggers who have had this happen, so the danger is very real.

Choose images from WikiCommons, Wikimedia, Pixabay, Unsplash, Morguefile or one of the other free photo sharing sites. Kristen Lamb's group My WANA (We Are Not Alone) has images that are free to use as long as you give attribution.

But don't make your site look too busy. Often one featured image is enough.

Keep your blog design simple and easy to read. That means no gray text on a slightly grayer background, or a font so tiny nobody over 40 can read it.

And avoid a black background. Yes, even though you write vampire detective fiction. Besides looking like an interface from 1987, light on dark is hard on the eyeballs. Ditto images behind the text. Anything too busy will drive people away, so go pretty minimalist with your images and design.

And give us lots of white space. I know I keep mentioning it, but white space is essential to readability on the Web. It makes your piece look like a breezy, easy read instead of a dense slog.

12) Put in Hyperlinks.

I happened to have done this right by mistake. (It's my academic training: write those footnotes! Cite your source!) I always link to my source material from the blog, so people don't think I'm making stuff up.

It turns out those hyperlinks are golden. They're how Google finds you. That's the bait that lures their spiders to your site—an essential part of SEO.

You are also doing a favor to other bloggers when you post hyperlinks to their sites. That's called a "backlink." If a spider happens to land on your blog first, it will lead them to your friend's blog. The number of backlinks, or "sites linking in" to a site factor into a website's ranking. They also alert the blogs you've linked to (in WordPress this is called a "pingback") and those bloggers may in return discover your site.

So good hyperlinks help everybody.

11—What Should You Blog About?

The most common question I get from authors who are thinking about starting a blog is: "What should I blog about?"

My answer isn't the same as what you hear from the business bloggers.

The business blog gurus will tell you to find a niche and stick with it.

But if you're blogging to promote a career as an author, forget niches and just be yourself.

Your blog subject matter should depend on your genre and where you are in your career. Of course, first you need to get that career started. When you're a newbie, your blogging goals will be different from those of an established author.

• An established author is blogging for fans and readers that already exist.

• A newbie is blogging to meet people and network.

The New Writer

If you're an unpublished or newly-published author/blogger, your primary goal is: get your name out there.

Start by networking with other bloggers. Fellow writers can be your best resource early in your career. Note: I'm not telling you to market to your fellow writers. When you're starting out, you're not marketing; you're networking.

Visit blogs that focus on your genre—that's readers, reviewers and other authors—to see what they're blogging about and get to know them. When you find yourself leaving a long comment: that's your next blog post!

A great place to network is the award-winning Insecure Writers Support Group, founded by sci-fi author Alex J. Cavanaugh. Joining in one of their blog hops will help you meet a lot of fellow bloggers.

I also recommend Nathan Bransford's Blog and forum, and Kristen Lamb's Blog and her "We Are Not Alone" website. Both are great for networking.

If you're planning on a traditional publishing career, you should also be regularly visiting agents' blogs—especially the ones who rep your genre—and you can network with writers in the query process at Query Tracker dot net and Agent Query dot com.

Visiting blogs can be like hanging out with co-workers in the coffee room at a new job. You'll find a huge amount of information just by listening. Think of your blog as your cubicle where people stop by to say hello. But first you have to introduce yourself in a general meeting place.

This means yes, you can talk about writing and publishing when you're starting out. You can commiserate and congratulate each other as you ride the roller coaster of this crazy business. (But no whining. Trash-talking people in the business can stop your career before it starts.)

The Published Author

Once you're published, it's time to switch gears. You don't have to stop blogging about writing entirely, but mix it up so you can start attracting more non-writers—especially readers in your genre. (Again, do as I say, not as I do, unless you're also putting out nonfiction books for writers like this one.)

Remember, people surf the Web looking for two things: information and entertainment.

Your blog can spin a good yarn, make people laugh, provide information, or all three, as long as you put it in your own honest, unique voice and you're not too whiny or preachy. You want to provide a way for people to relate to you on a personal level.

Of course, first you need to know who you're blogging for. If you're writing hard sci-fi, you're going to want to reach a different readership than if you're writing cozy mysteries or romance.

Try picturing your ideal audience when you're deciding what to blog about. What movies and TV shows might appeal to people who would like your book? What's their age group? What other interests do those people have?

If you're writing Y.A. dystopian, blogging about the most recent films in the genre might attract your ideal demographic. Tweet news about the stars and whether or not there will be a sequel, and you'll get those fans coming to your blog.

Write mysteries? Discuss classic mysteries or all the retellings of the Sherlock Holmes stories in film and new books. Or the latest BBC mystery you're watching on Acorn.

If you're writing Regency romance, run a series on your favorite films set in the era, or talk costumes and history. Or conduct a survey on what actor was the ideal Darcy.

Topics for an Author Blog

This is by necessity a partial list. I hope it will give you some ideas that will spark your own writer's imagination.

Profiles and Interviews

These don't have to be interviews with authors, although that's a fantastic way to network as well as reach readers.

- Write crime novels? Interview a cop, forensic expert or private detective.
- Write bookstore cozies? Profile a series of bookstore clerks and visit their blogs.
- Write wine country romances? Talk to vintners, tasting room workers, local chefs.

Any time you write a post about somebody other than yourself, you bring those people—and their friends—to your site.

Lists of Chosen Links

Do you surf the Web looking for articles and blogposts on your favorite subjects? Collect the URL's of the best ones and recommend them in a regular list on your blog.

This is one of the best ways of getting to know top bloggers. Put them on a list and they'll get a Google alert and stop by your blog. Maybe they'll even invite you to guest post. And if you recommend a lesser-known blogger...you've made a friend!

Some blogs that have great curated lists are Joel Friedlander's "This Week in Blogs" and Elizabeth S. Craig's Sunday "Twitterific." (Both valuable resources for all writers.)

Information Pieces

This is where you can use all that research you did for your books that sounds too much like "info-dumping" in your novel. Get it out of your novel and onto a blog!

Reviews and Spotlights of Books in Your Genre.

Reviews are hard work and sometimes a thankless job, but good reviewers get a lot of respect in the industry.

Spotlights are easier, so you might want to intersperse them. A "spotlight" simply gives the book blurb, author bio and links to the book's buy pages without a lengthy review. It's understood you recommend the book, but you don't have to go into details about why.

Listicles

"Top 10" lists are always popular, and you can compile them on subjects related to your books. If you write a romance set in an exotic locale, you can write the "10 Romantic Getaway Spots." If you've written a children's book about a toy or plush animal, you can write "14 Toys in Kid Lit." And there's always "Top 10 Books..." in your genre or whatever.

Lists are fun and easy to read, so they get a lot of traffic. You can list any number, but research says anything over twenty sounds like too much work to most people, and ten is the most popular.

Film Reviews and Reviews of Other Media in Your Genre

Readers are interested in more than books, so talking about films and television shows in your genre will draw readers.

Comic or Inspirational Stories about Your Life

This can be almost anything, as long as it's entertaining, has a point, and doesn't turn into a pity party. It can be that series of personal essays you plan to turn into a memoir later.

Stuff about Your Pets.

Never underestimate the power of a cute puppy or grumpy cat to draw readers. Especially if animals play an important part in your fiction. Funny stories and pictures about animals will get lots of play on Facebook, Pinterest, and Instagram and bring people to your blog.

Opinions (Especially Funny Ones.)

Do avoid polarizing subjects unless that's part of your brand, but any opinion piece about publishing news or book events will probably get a lot of readers in the book community. An opinion blog I love these days is hilarious Irish writer Tara Sparling's blog. She can make you laugh about everything from Amazon's latest catastrophic decision, to dealing with infuriating bureaucrats at the Russian Embassy.

Nostalgia and Historical Pieces.

Do you write historical romances or novels set in an earlier era? Anything about that era will be of interest to your readers. Write about clothing, homes, or customs of your era or region. Photos are a big plus here.

This is where people writing books of military history or memorabilia can share their own experiences. If you lived through history, the world wants to know about it. A blog is the perfect place to share, especially if you have photos.

Travel Pieces.

These can be about where you live, travel, or the settings of your books.

Even if you've only made the journey via Google maps and Wikipedia, your readers will be interested. (Remember to be careful to use only photos you've taken yourself or images that are out of copyright.)

If the setting of your books is your own hometown, even better. Interview local business owners and people who live and work in similar places to your fictional ones.

Recipes and Crafting Instructions.

Write crafting mysteries? Offer interesting quilt patterns or knitting directions. Have a character who likes to fly kites? Tell readers how to build one. And no matter what genre you write, if food is involved, people will enjoy a recipe for it.

Or maybe you can offer a recipe for the busy writer to throw in the crockpot, or a tasty snack to serve to your book group.

Anything of Interest to Your Demographic.

Anything that might make a good magazine article will make a good blogpost—especially a magazine your ideal reader is likely to buy.

Treat a blog as an expression of who you are as a writer and have fun with it. Your blog is the face you offer the world.
***

Think of your blog as something like your own version of Oprah's magazine. It can be any collection of eclectic things that add up to you.

12—What Not to Blog About

Remember your blog is the face you present to the world. It's your home on the Web, but it's more like the front parlor, not the den where you let it all hang out. So be on your best behavior.

The following topics can fizzle a blog, so mention them sparingly, if at all.

Word Count on Your WIP

Sorry. Nobody cares. (Unless you're a member of a writers' group encouraging each other on—as sometimes happens during NaNoWriMo—National Novel Writing Month.)

Rejections and Bad Reviews

Resist posting rants about the unfairness of the publishing industry. Or how lame that famous writer's work is compared to yours. Or how a famous writer somehow must have hacked into your computer and stolen your idea, because you thought of it *first*.

I'm amazed at how many newbie writers think people are stealing their ideas. There are only so many plots. New writers value ideas much more than seasoned authors.

Veteran authors know it's not about the idea—it's about how many hours you spend with your butt in the chair and hands on the keyboard.

It's okay when you've had a big disappointment to ask for

the emotional support of your friends, but don't give specifics and never rail against the agent / editor / reviewer who spurned you.

Remember the first thing an agent will do if she's interested in your query is Google you. She probably just had lunch with that editor you called Miss Poop-for-Brains.

This stuff belongs in your private journal. The one with the lock on it.

Blogs need to be "other" oriented rather than "self" oriented. That means you need to write stuff that's interesting to people who don't already know you.

Writer's Block.

Ditto. I'll swear 90% of the blogposts on Medium are about writer's block. Boring. If you don't have anything to say, don't say it. Go to the beach. Or the library. I believe Writer's Block is real, but so is Writer's Boredom. Sometimes all you need is a break. What you don't want is to spread that boredom around.

Professorial Teaching

Especially if you're not an expert. Don't lecture people on how to get published if you're not. Or tell people how to self-publish if you've only published one book and don't know the difference between a publisher and a book distributor, as one newbie on Medium did recently.

If you write nonfiction, you're blogging to establish yourself as an authority, so make sure you back up your statements with links and do your research.

How You Haven't Been Blogging.

All those business blog gurus tell you to post once a day or even more, but remember their advice isn't aimed at creative writers. We have other priorities. So don't apologize or make excuses.

I'm actually relieved when my favorite bloggers cut back a bit on regular posting. That way I have some hope of keeping up.

But I see apologies for not blogging all the time. Some blogger hasn't made his own self-imposed deadline and then spends half of his post apologizing for it to no one in particular.

We know it's hard to get around to the old blog. You don't need to tell us the specifics. Just call it "slow blogging" and get on with something interesting. (The slow blogging movement is like the "slow food" movement: quality over quantity.)

Joining the "slow blog" movement is simple. Next time you miss a few deadlines, tell yourself you didn't fail to blog; you succeeded in joining the slow bloggers. All you have to do is skip those boring apologies, and you're in.

Blogging slowly means it will take you longer to get into the search engines, but most blogs burn out after three years, and you want yours to be a platform to support you for the long haul.

Writing about Writing (Exclusively)

It's tempting to start a blog that caters to writers. But it's not that great an idea unless you write books *for* writers. I know it may seem that everybody and his grandmother is writing a book, but limiting your audience to writers is going to put big damper on sales later on. I'm speaking from experience here.

Controversial Stuff, Especially Politics

Unless your work is only for people of the same faith or political persuasion, you're eliminating a big percentage of the population by posting about controversial stuff.

I know some big name authors have been expressing their political opinions on their blogs recently, but it's a bad idea for newbies.

Unless, of course, your books are about religion or politics — or you live in a part of the world with interesting politics and you have a unique viewpoint. (Extra credit if you're in a war zone.)

Your Novel-in-Progress

You can write *about* your current project, but don't compose a novel on your blog.

Make sure everything you post has a purpose beyond begging for praise. If you do post creative work, ask for criticism (although writing forums are better for this) or use it as an example of how you worked out a knotty problem.

Also, remember the publishing establishment is wary of novels that have been "previously published" on a blog, because for novels, platform isn't as important as the size of a potential audience.

Nonfiction books can be composed on a blog as long as they're not cut and pasted word for word into a book. As I mentioned earlier, Amazon is cracking down on books that have "content that's freely available on the web."

But for novels, it's not a good idea. Even if you're planning to avoid the publishing establishment and self-publish that novel, don't write it in public.

Remember every novel needs careful pacing. Rough drafts are never perfectly paced and often take detours that need to be deleted later. Your future self will thank you for not publishing an iffy first draft. Remember the Internet is forever.

As I said earlier, if you want to write your novel in public and get feedback, Wattpad is probably the best place to do that. It is password protected and posting there is generally not considered officially "publishing" by most people in the industry. (However some agents now consider a book that's been on Wattpad to be "previously published," so do it at your own risk.)

Meandering

"Today I went to the dentist, then picked up some groceries and cooked my husband's favorite meatloaf," will snoozify anybody who isn't a member of your immediate family. Remember this isn't a daily diary.

And I'll remind you not to use an author blog as a journal of your personal emotional ups and downs. You want your blog to express your professional self, not your sweatpants-and-bunny-slippers self. Especially if you don't have a gift for humor. Keep in mind that everything you say is "in public" and Google will remember it forever.

A blog is like a magazine. You don't want to show yourself warts and all. You want to show your polished, professional persona.

Focusing on One Book

Posting cute observations from your character's point of view seems clever and fun. But it can get old fast. Plus it will limit the scope of your blog.

Yes, I know some bloggers have managed to sustain this kind of *tour de force* for a while — but what happens when you get a publisher and your editor has you change the character's name? Or that series doesn't sell and you move on to something else?

You want a blog to establish your career — not lock you into a box.

You're going to write more than one book, right? So you don't want to limit yourself to your current WIP, especially if you're unpublished.

When choosing topics for your blog, think outside the book. Talk about things that interest your readers, but not necessarily about your own writing.

13—Writing Your Author Bio

The author bio on your blog or website is probably the most important piece of writing you'll post on the Web, so you want to put some thought into it. It's what is going to define you for agents, editors, journalists, bloggers, and anybody else who may want to do business with you.

If you're a beginner, you may still be afraid to tell more than a handful of people you're a writer. And maybe you feel pretentious calling yourself an "author."

But it's time to start.

So, write it now. Yes. Right now. Before you start that blog. Even if you've never published anything but the Halloween haiku that won second prize in your high school newspaper.

Actually, you want to write two bios: 1) a paragraph suitable for those online profiles like Gravatar, or a magazine byline, and 2) a longer one-page version for posting on your "About Me" page (and sending to agents and editors who still ask for a separate bio.)

The One-Page Author Bio

Use a professional photo of yourself here. Preferably the same one you used in your online profile. Title the bio only with your name. It may seem clever to write "Who the #%@& is this Guy?" Or "Who is this Moron?" As I've seen with several newbie writers, but professionalism is what you want here.

Write in the third person. Keep to about 250 words.

You're aiming for a style similar to book jacket copy. The purpose is to make yourself sound professional and interesting.

This may be perfectly accurate: "Mrs. H. O. Humm is a stay-at-home mom who lives in Middle America with her dentist husband, 2.4 children and a dog named Rex."

But a bio is all about making yourself stand out. So say something more like: "Hermione Oz Humm was born in the Emerald City and is an expert balloonist, ventriloquist and voice-over performer."

Things to consider including:
Whatever Might Make You Newsworthy

Okay, so you aren't the baby who got rescued from that well forty years ago, and you never dated a celebrity or a politician, but whatever is quirky or unusual about you, trot it out. Keep homing pigeons? Run marathons? Cook prize-winning chili? Put it in.

Work History

Here's where you say you're a welder or a fourth grade teacher or whatever, even if it isn't related to the subject matter of your book.

NOTE: Don't call yourself a "novelist" if you haven't yet published one. "Writer" is better.

If you're seriously under-employed and want to keep it to yourself, you can call yourself a "freelance writer," but consider saying what else you do, even if it's less than impressive. I remember when Christopher Moore's first book, *Practical Demonkeeping*, came out and all our newspapers ran stories about how a "local waiter" had just sold a book to Disney. If he'd called himself a "writer" there would have been no story.

Where You Live

Your hometown might make a good focus for marketing. Every area has its quirks and fun stories. Plus people like to be able to picture you in your native habitat.

"Susie Scrivener is not a fan of broccoli, although she lives in Santa Maria, California, the broccoli capital of the world" is a fun fact that could make good copy.

Education

This includes workshops or writers' conferences as well as formal education—especially if you worked with a high-profile teacher. If you took a playwriting workshop with Edward Albee, even if it was 30 years ago, go ahead and say so.

Life Experience and Hobbies

Especially if they relate to the book. But anything's good that can fascinate on its own: If you collect vintage Frisbees, and the book is about angsty teen werewolves at a Frisbee contest, include it.

If you invented the Frisbee, it doesn't matter what your book is about: toot that horn!

Travel/Exotic Residences

"Rudy Kipling once took a two-week tour of Asia," meh. But "Mr. Kipling was born in Bombay and spent a year as the assistant editor of a newspaper in Lahore," is something people will want to know.

Writing Credentials/Prizes

Here's where you can list some of those credits in small presses and prizes that people say will clutter up a query.

Also include any books you've published, plays you've had produced, poetry slams you've won, whatever. It doesn't matter if they're not in the genre you're writing in now.

Family: Use Discretion Here.

If you write for children and have some of your own, it would be useful to mention them. If your family has an interesting claim to fame (like your sister just won an Olympic medal or works in the White House) do tell us about it. And if family history has made you uniquely qualified to write this book (Your grandfather was Dwight Eisenhower's valet and you're writing about the Eisenhower/Kay Summersby affair) that's golden.

But don't invade your family's privacy any more than you have to. Especially your children's privacy. Don't post their photos or let people know where they go to school unless it's absolutely necessary. Remember the Internet is full of predators and trolls. You may be physically in the privacy of your own home when you post, but everything you put on your blog is "in public."

Performing History

It's helpful to show you're not paralyzed by the thought of public speaking. You can mention you're the vice president of your local Toastmasters, or host a jug band program on a public access station, or you played the teapot in last year's production of *Beauty and the Beast* at the local community theater.

These are fun things that make you relatable, plus they might get you some invitations to guest on podcasts, writer's conferences, or other speaking engagements.

Your Online Presence

Don't forget to include your social media links so people can follow and friend you.

The One-Paragraph Author Bio

This is the one to include with your guest posts.

Again, write in the third person. For the first sentence, this format works pretty well:

"[Your Name] is a _____ who lives in _____ and does _____."

Then you can add one or two of the following:

Is a member of _____ (if you're a member of any writing organizations like RWA, Sisters in Crime, or SCBWI)

Has won_____ (writing awards — yes, you can mention the Halloween haiku.)

Was published in _____ .

Has a degree in _____ from_____.

Then add something interesting and unique about yourself, preferably something related to the piece, like:

"S/he played Glinda the Good Witch in a Middle School production of *The Wizard of Oz.*"

When writing these bios, think like a reporter. What would make good copy in a news release? Think unique, quirky, or funny.

Having these bios ready to send out or post whenever necessary will save you stress later on.

14—How to Start that Blog in 18 Easy Steps

Creating a blog isn't as hard as you may think, even if you're a cybermoron like me.

Again, forget all that techy business blog advice.

As an author, you want your blog to be a personal, inviting place where people can visit and get to know you—a home rather than a storefront. But that doesn't need to be anything complicated.

Okay, so you've been reading blogs and commenting on them and you have an online profile (see Chapters #6 and #7.)

Now you're ready to start your very own blog.

Tech people usually assume everybody knows the basics, which is why the basics are the hardest part to figure out if you're brand new to all this.

So here they are:

1) Visit Other Blogs.

If you haven't done it yet, spend a couple of weeks reading a bunch of blogs in your genre before you jump in and create your own. See what you like and don't like.

Also, visit some agent blogs and/or popular indie-publishing blogs. These are great for meeting people who can help you get started and answer some of your questions.

2) Write Drafts of a Few Posts.

For possible blog topics, review Chapter #11, "What Should an Author Blog About" and you might also want to peek at Chapter #15 "How to Write Blog Content."

Here are some handy things to keep in mind before you compose your first drafts.

- The ideal length is about 1000-1500 words presented in short, punchy paragraphs. Longer is okay if it's all on one subject (Our posts are usually about 2500 words) and shorter is fine as long as it's over 300 words.
- Bulleting, numbering, and bolding keep the reader's eye moving.
- Make a point and present it in a way that's easy to grasp.
- Offer information and interesting observations, not navel-gazing. Direct your focus outward, not inward.
- If you have more to say than fits into the word count—great! You have material for next time.
- Keep to one topic, because that stimulates conversation more effectively.

3) Choose a Blogging Platform.

The biggest free blogging platforms are WordPress (dot com) and Blogger. Tumblr is a platform for short posts, videos and pictures—something between a blog and Twitter. Weebly is a website builder that's easy to use and has a no-frills blog function. And as I wrote in Chapter #9, Medium is a basic blogging site where you can't personalize, so I don't recommend it as your main blog, although it's great for extending your reach.

There are other excellent blogging platforms like SquareSpace, which has great tech support, but they don't have a free option as of this writing.

You can also have a blog on your personal website, or on a writer's forum like Goodreads. But these aren't as likely to be picked up by search engine spiders, so if your goal is to be more Google-able, I suggest using a more popular platform.

I used Blogger for six years and liked it fine. (It's owned by Google, with addresses that read "Blogspot dot com.") It's the easiest to set up and use — and has some nice templates.

But Blogger does have drawbacks. There's no tech support, so you have to rely on forums to ask advice of more experienced bloggers. Also, a lot of decisions are made for you, and you don't have a lot of choices. But almost anybody can figure out how to use it.

People who are more tech-savvy love WordPress. And now that I know how to use it, I love it, too. But it's a steep learning curve for people like me who weren't born to the tech world.

There are two kinds of WordPress blog: WordPress dot com and WordPress dot org. The dot com is free for the basic version, which works fine for most authors. It doesn't support ads or sales, which isn't a problem for author bloggers. WordPress can also grow with your career, and you can buy "plug ins" and get more security later.

Blogger is easier and more intuitive, but you have a lot less choice. If that works for you, Blogger may be a good choice. As I said, it worked fine for me for many years.

4) Decide on a Focus and Tone.

Remember you can change these, so have some fun here. Generally you want to choose something in keeping with what you write. Pink hearts and lace probably won't work for dark thrillers and creepy black branches against a purple sky won't draw readers for your beachy rom-coms.

If you haven't settled on a genre, or you write several, choose something that expresses your personality instead of one type of writing.

I know a popular author who started out as a Y.A. writer and switched to erotic romance. Yeah, a tough switch — but she changed the look and tone of the blog and it worked.

Beginning author-bloggers form a wonderful community. That community can help you in hundreds of ways, so don't worry too much about seeming like an experienced blogger right away. Be real, flexible, open, and friendly and you can ease into your niche later.

Remember the most successful blogs reveal the writer's personality and provide something useful at the same time.

Note for erotica authors: If you decide to go the erotica or steamy romance route: clearly mark adult content. If your content contains explicit erotica or extreme violence, make sure you have a portal where the reader can say if he/she is over 18. You can't keep them from lying, of course, but this will warn visitors and allow parental controls to work.

5) Think of a Title and Tag Line.

Don't get too creative here. As I've said, make sure you put your own name in the title. Your name is your brand.

Anywhere you go in social media, you want to be promoting your brand. Otherwise you're wasting time. (That's time you could be writing that opus that's the reason for all this, remember?) It's OK to be unimaginative like me and call it Your Name's Blog—maybe reducing the ho-hum factor with something like "Susie Smith, Scrivener."

Also, don't put your book title in the blog title, since hopefully, you'll be writing more books. And if you don't want to get locked into one genre, keep the genre out of the title too. You want to keep the blog as flexible as possible.

But you can have more fun with the "tag line", or sub-header

Our blog is officially "Anne R. Allen's Blog...with Ruth Harris. Writing about Writing. Mostly."

"Writing about writing. Mostly." is the tag line.

So instead of calling your blog "Musing, Meandering and Muttering," call it "Susie Smith, Author" and use "Musing, Meandering and muttering" as your tag line.

6) Choose Images to Set Tone and Illustrate the Blog.

Usually you want one of yourself for your profile, and another image to set the tone in the header. And of course you'll want to display your book covers and link to your buy pages if you have books for sale. Try to keep with the same color scheme and tone in both photos.

Anywhere you're on social media, aim to echo the tone and color on your home page in order to establish a personal "brand" look.

A blog isn't Instagram or Pinterest, so images shouldn't be your main focus. You're a writer and you're blogging to promote your writing skills, not your skills as a photographer, presumably.

But you will need images for each blogpost, so start collecting those copyright-free images that either you take yourself or get from free image sharing sites on the Web. (There's more on images in Chapter #10.)

7) Prepare a Bio for Your "About Me" Page.

As I said in Chapter #13, this is the most important part of the blog. It doesn't have to be as short as the bios you send to agents or put on social media sites, so have fun with it.

Make it intriguing and fun without over-sharing. You can add some more pics here—maybe of your dog or your funky car. Again I suggest keeping family out unless it's a parenting blog. Pseudonyms for kids are a smart idea for protecting their privacy.

8) Go to a Friend's Blog and Click on "Create Blog."

If your friend uses Blogger or WordPress, there will be a link at the top that says "create blog."

Follow directions in the window. They're pretty easy. Medium is easiest, Blogger is easy, too, and if you have trouble, just go to "Support.Google.com/Blogger" and look for "How to Use Blogger." WordPress is a little harder, but there are good directions at WordPress.com for "How to Set up Your Blog."

9) Choose a Template or Theme.

Don't mess with the provided template or theme too much, except in terms of color—a busy blog isn't a place people want to linger. And don't add animation, GIFs, huge files, or anything that takes too long to load. Keep with your color scheme and tone.

WordPress themes are more involved than Blogger templates. Make sure you choose one that's simple enough for you to work with.

10) Pick Your "Widgets" or "Gadgets."

There are lots. But again, keep it simple. I suggest just choosing the basics like "about me" , "subscribe" , "share" , "search this blog" and "followers" if you're on Blogger. ("Followers" are people who follow the blog in an RSS feed, not email subscribers.)

The "followers" widget is fun because you get to see the faces of everybody who's following. It can be exciting to see your follower list grow. But don't get discouraged. At the beginning you won't have many. Just accept that as part of the process and don't obsess.

"Share" is the collection of buttons that allow readers to Tweet your post or send it to Instagram, Facebook, Pinterest etc.

You can go back and add any other widgets you want later.

In a little while, if you have Blogger, you'll want to install the "Popular Post" gadget that lists your posts that have the most traffic. That makes people want to move around the site, so they don't leave after they've only read one post.

I don't recommend putting your stats on the front page for "so many hits" or whatever. Like the followers widget, it will only advertise that you're a newbie, and there's no real purpose to it. The followers widget allows people to follow you. "So many hits" doesn't do much of anything except tell how many third world spammers have tried to get into the blog.

Do keep track of your stats on your own dashboard, but remember it takes about a year to get a blog going at full stride. Yes, you will have weeks when you have two hits. My first blog had five hits in its first three months.

But checking stats is a good idea, because you can see where your traffic is coming from. If you suddenly get forty hits from one address — go check it out. Somebody's probably posted a link to you. You may have a new friend you didn't even know about.

A word about subscriptions: Blogger provides ways for people to follow you either by subscription or through the follower widget, which, as I mentioned earlier, means your new posts will go into the subscriber's RSS feed.

But it's better to get people to subscribe to email notifications. That way they'll always get the notices.

Make sure you place that subscription widget in a prominent spot on your sidebar. The upper right corner is considered prime real estate on a Web page.

After you have a bunch of subscribers, you may want to switch to a separate mail program like MailChimp, so you'll have the names and addresses of your subscribers and can keep track of the numbers, but that's not necessary when you're just starting out.

11) Set up Comment Settings.

You set these up through the "Settings" menu. In WordPress, there's a separate section for "Discussion" under "Settings."

As I've said, I suggest making no restrictions on comments on new posts. Don't make every comment wait for your approval before it goes live. You won't get a discussion going that way.

Some people choose to put on a "CAPTCHA" (the I-am-not-a-robot thingy) to restrict robo-spam, but your spamblocker will usually catch the robots, and a CAPTCHA does nothing to deter trolls. It can also annoy real commenters, so it's not a great idea. A CAPTCHA used to be automatically installed on a Blogger blog, and you had to disable it, but they no longer do that.

It's best to monitor your blog yourself. I've personally found that 99% of commenters are friendly, and it takes spammers and trolls a while to find your blog.

But DO have comments over a week old sent to you for moderation. Old posts are most likely to attract spam. (But if you do get spam, make sure you tag it as spam to train your spamblocker to block it.)

12) Sign up for Email Notifications of New Comments

You want to respond to them as soon as you can. If commenters give an email address in their profile (always smart) you can respond to them via email, but it's much better to respond in the comment thread to stimulate discussion.

Do this through your "Settings" menu. Blogger allows you to list ten email addresses where you can be notified.

13) Upload those Photos.

If you're on Blogger, just click on the icon of a picture frame in your toolbar. In WordPress, there's a button that says "Add Media." There will be an option to add information and/or links to the photos.

Do caption the photos and add "alt attributes" in WordPress. "Alt" attributes, short for "alternative attributes" describe the photo so that screen readers for the blind can describe the photo. Use your main keyword in the description—that's good for SEO.

Again don't feel you have to go nuts with images. Yes, you need them, but unless you're a photographer or travel writer, the writing is your central focus. The main thing is to make sure it's over 300 pixels in each direction, otherwise it may not be picked up by social media.

14) BOOKMARK Your blog.

This is important. Otherwise, you may never find it again. You'd be amazed how many people set up a blog only to have it disappear forever into cyberspace. I did it myself. Google is not going be able to help you find it until you've been blogging for a while.

When you go back to your blog, if you're on Blogger and you're signed into Google (which you will be if you have Gmail) you get into the blog by clicking on "design" in the upper right corner of the toolbar. If you're not signed in, that button will simply say "sign in."

15) Sign up for Google Alerts on Your Blog Title.

As an author, you also want to sign up for Google Alerts on your own name and your published book titles, so if you haven't signed up for those alerts, do them at the same time. You just go to "Google Alerts" and sign up.

Google Alerts are supposed to tell you every time somebody mentions your name or blog anywhere on the Web. Sometimes they don't, and Google can be very odd in what it picks up, but when the alerts work, they can be very useful.

They'll tell you if somebody has mentioned your blog, so you can go visit and see who's talking about you and (if it's safe) join in the conversation. If the remarks are snarky or mean, you may not want to join in the discussion. If they've misunderstood you, you might want to send a private message. Otherwise, just ignore them. (But remember the names. It's good to know your enemies.)

Badmouthing doesn't happen all that often. It's much more likely you'll find somebody recommended your blog and you may have made a friend.

16) Decide on a Schedule.

It's good to decide how often you want to blog before you start. As I've said, I suggest once a week to start — then do it. You will get more traction with the search engines if you post more often, and as I've said, you may want to start out posting several times a week to get started.

Most blog gurus will tell you to blog three times a week, minimum, but I have never blogged more than twice in one week and my stats are fine.

But do plan to post to your blog on the same day each week.

17) Go Tell Those Blog-Pals you've made that you've got a Blog.

Hopefully, a few will come by and follow you. Don't despair if you don't get a lot of followers right away. I had maybe ten for my first six months—consisting of my critique group and my mom.

18) Congratulations. You are now a Blogger!

Really. It's that easy.

15—Writing Blog Content

So you've got a blog. Congratulations. You are now a "content provider." Sounds a lot more technical than "writer" doesn't it?

In some ways it is. Writing Web content isn't exactly the same as traditional writing for an essay or a magazine article.

According to Mike Blankenship, writing for Smart Blogger, the paragraph has gone through radical changes in the past 10 years. He says the 100-200 word standard paragraph has disappeared. Now your average paragraph should be between two and four lines. You can go over and under — some paragraphs are just one word long — but stay close to that average and you should be fine. But don't make them all the same length. Mike says, "Switching between short and long paragraphs will make your writing sing."

Learning Web Content Writing is Mostly Unlearning.

I had to unlearn a whole lot of what I was taught about writing prose back in the 20th century in order to be an effective content provider. (Thanks to my first online editor, Daryl Jung at *Inkwell Newswatch*.)

Back in the 20th century, good writers…

- Learned to use topic sentences and avoid cutting to a new paragraph until there's a new topic.
- Wrote for people who paid money for our words and read every one.
- Wouldn't put a title on a serious essay that looked like a

cheap tabloid headline.

- Avoided repetition.
- Would never offer an outline instead of an essay.
- Substantiated information with footnotes.
- Never heard of tags, keywords, or SEO.

But the majority of people don't read on the Internet; they skim. In fact, most people don't even skim the whole article. Recently, Farhad Manjoo reported in *Slate* that only half the people who visit a site read past the first hundred words.

So how do you get them to come by...and stay?

Throw out the rules you learned in school and use a copywriter's tricks for grabbing your audience and not letting them go. Here are some copywriting techniques you might want to add to your writing skill set.

Learn to Write Enticing Headers

Yes, I'm harping on this a lot. But this is the most important aspect of learning to blog.

Author C. Hope Clark once said in her "Funds for Writers" newsletter:

"You might be surprised at the key factor I use in deleting or holding to read: The quality of the subject line. Hey, when time is crazy limited...the words have to snag me as I rush by. That means first and foremost that the subject be crisp, sharp, attractive, intriguing, or whatever adjective you want to use that gives me whiplash. It has to shout, "HEY, READ ME OR YOU'LL REGRET IT."

She's right. Headers are the most important element of your blog content, and it's the one most novelists don't get. We want our blogs to sound creative and literary like our books, not cheesy like a supermarket tabloid.

But tabloid and advertising writers know what they're doing. They have only a moment to grab a reader going through that checkout line, so they need an irresistible hook.

In our case, headers need to make Tweets and shares that will snag a reader in the endless stream of content they can choose from.

So how do we do that?

Make a Header Tweetable

That means avoiding enigmatic, one-word headers. I recently saw a title in the *London Review of Books* that exemplified the one-word header that doesn't work well in the age of Twitter. The article was called "Ghosting." It turned out to be about Andrew O'Hagan's experience ghostwriting for Julian Assange, a fascinating subject.

But you wouldn't know from the title. It might have been a piece on bad boyfriends who evaporate, or ectoplasmic apparitions, or the TV show with Adam Scott and Craig Robinson. So I didn't bother to Retweet it since I didn't have time to write a new header. You don't want that to happen to your posts.

Promise a Speedy Read

Everybody's in a hurry online.

Author Jillian Mullin wrote in the *Web Writer Spotlight*:

"Generally, an average web user only spends 10 to 30 seconds reading Internet content. People rarely read web pages word-per-word. Instead, they scan the page for related keywords, bullet points, subtitles, and quotes."

One of the best ways to let people know you've got a quick, easy-scan piece is with a numbered "listicle" like "The 10 Best Ghostwritten Books" or "Five Signs Your Computer is Possessed."

Stir Emotions or Offer Useful advice

- You can sensationalize: "Why This Woman is Afraid of her own Apartment!"
- Or appeal to sentiment: "This Story of a Talented Cat Will Melt Your Heart."
- Stir up some greed: "How Wendy Writer inked a 7-Figure Deal with her Haunted Apartment Story."
- Or paranoia: "Is Your Cubicle Haunted?" Or "Who or WHAT is Flushing Your Toilet in the Middle of the Night?"

- Or simple curiosity: "10 Things You Don't Know about Poltergeists."
- Or appeal to thriftiness: "Save Money and Time with a Do-It-Yourself Exorcism."

Pack Your First Words with Essential Info

Make sure your most important info is visible as soon as somebody opens your blog. People do a lot of reading on phones and small tablets these days, so those first words are all-important for today's reader.

It's also what Google shows in the search results. And those opening words will help the spiders decide what searches will pick it up, so you need some keywords there, too.

And since most people won't read past the second paragraph, you don't want to save your best stuff for the end. Half a century ago, journalists were taught to "humanize" stories by starting with a human interest line.

"Wendy Writer shouldn't have a care in the world. She's a pretty thirty-something freelance writer living in a gorgeous Victorian triplex in Old Town. She's sitting on the front porch of the house she moved into last month with her cat Hortense. The three-story home was once owned by one Mildred Biggins, who died in 1924..."

The reporter could wait to get to the lead (then known as the "lede" to differentiate from the metal originally used to make type) in the third or fourth sentence, but these days, you've got to give us the facts in the first 50-60 characters.

50-60 characters. That's all Google shows in the search results, so make these words work hard.

It's also what will show in any preview that appears on Facebook or other social media, so you don't want to save any "good stuff" for later.

Just say it: "Wendy Writer's house is haunted by the ghost of Mildred Biggins."

Use and Properly Format Sub-headers

Sub-headers are essential for drawing traffic and keeping it. They have three jobs:

- Emphasize your important points.
- Draw the eye through the piece.
- Include keywords and signal your topics to search engines.

So if you're writing about Mildred Biggins, you want to use sub-headers that contain words like " ghost" , "haunted" , and "poltergeist" , rather than "Flappers in the Night" or " Mildred or Hortense...who's Flushing the Toilet at 3 AM?" .

IMPORTANT: Be sure to use the "header" and "sub-header" mode in your blog program, and not the "normal" or "paragraph" setting.

For Blogger users, the sub-header menu is on the left-hand side of the toolbar, where you see the word "normal." That window has a menu, where you can choose Heading, Subheading, or Minor Heading.

For WordPress users, it's in the menu where you see "paragraph" as the default setting. You can choose "Headings" from one down to six.

When I started blogging, I didn't have a clue about formatting, and didn't know that "spiders" don't recognize "normal" text as a sub-header even if it looks like one to human eyes. Finally somebody told me about the importance of using the appropriate format and our blog stats soared.

Break up Blocks of Text

You want to do whatever it takes to avoid big hunks of indigestible verbiage. Nothing is more daunting to a Web reader.

I subscribe to Publisher's Lunch, the daily report on traditional publishing's latest news. But like so much of traditional publishing, it's stuck in the 20th century. The information on new book deals comes in one big, passive-aggressive block of text in a tiny, gray, sans-serif font. I find myself dreading opening it every morning. Recently, I've just been skipping it.

Break up those word hunks! Forget what you learned in school about topic sentences. Don't write a paragraph more than a few sentences long.

I know. Your high school English teacher is rolling in her grave, but skimmers read the first sentence of a paragraph and maybe the last. Make your big points in those two spots.

Write in a Conversational Style

A blog is not the place to show off your encyclopedic vocabulary. If somebody has to click around to look up a word, they probably won't come back.

It's also not the place for jargon. Don't write in geekspeak, legalese, or that "most scholars agree" phony-tony style you learned to use for college term papers.

Many tech people write in a language comprehensible only to them. It identifies them as "in the know." But an "in crowd" blog isn't going to get as many followers as one that's friendly and welcoming to all.

Marketers and SEO specialists are some of the worst offenders. Several years ago, I remember being told I had to learn about something called Google Authorship. I read dozens of blogposts about it, but I couldn't figure out if it was a software program, an app, a Google Plus circle, or the name of Larry Page's cat. Nobody seemed able to define it. They only put people down who didn't have it.

A few years later, I read that Google Authorship had died. I couldn't help feeling it had something to do with the fact nobody outside of Google had any idea what it was.

You're not going to reach the general public if you write in geek-speak and act smug.

Write Easy-to-Skim Content

Skimming is easier with lists, bullet points, and bolding. Italics can be useful too—anything to draw the eye along the text.

MS Word makes this a breeze. Unfortunately a lot of

Word formatting probably won't translate to your blog program, so you may have to resort to primitive means like numbering your own lists or using asterisks for bullet points.

A numbered list has a three-fold benefit:

1. It provides lots of white space.
2. It draws the eye through.
3. It gives you fodder for your headline. (See the "header" section.)

Bullet points are good too.

- Like numbered lists, bullet points are easy to grasp at a glance and they let people know they're just getting the "good parts."
- **Bolding**: It's especially good for headers and other significant information.
- Italics: Putting a quote in italics sets it apart from the normal text.

Choose Informative Anchor Text for Hyperlinks

Hyperlinks are all-important in blogging.

What are hyperlinks? It's okay to ask. I had no idea how to make a hyperlink for the first six months I blogged.

You make a hyperlink when you turn an ugly URL like this: "http:// annerallen . com/ beware-bogus-literary-agents/ " into a live bit of text that you can click on to take you to that address.

You make a hyperlink by selecting the text (called "anchor text") that you want people to click on. Then you go to the icon that looks like two links of chain up there on the menu bar. Or in Blogger it is cleverly identified with the word "Link."

Don't make the link with the word "here" or "this link." That's because the words "here" and "this link" don't mean anything to the Google spiders.

So select the whole phrase and make the hyperlink to that. So you'd select the words, "Beware Bogus Literary Agents," and put in the URL to that post. (Like the ugly one above.)

Spiders only notice links with identifying text. So either use the title of the piece as I did above, or say something about it, like "the time agent Janet Reid visited my newbie author blog."

That gives me the added perk that somebody searching for info on newbie author blogs or agent Janet Reid might find my post.

Keep SEO in Mind, but Don't Lard Your Post with Repetitive Words

I know SEO is one of those jargon expressions that make most writers' eyes glaze over. A lot of people think it means repeating the same words over and over. But search engines actually favor using regular speech these days, so you don't usually need to do anything strange to "optimize" for a search engine.

All you need to do is use simple keywords to help Google and other search engines find you. The best way to optimize for search engines is check after you write your post to see if you have keywords in the following:

- Headline
- First paragraph
- Sub-headers
- Anchor text for hyperlinks.
- Tags

And don't worry a lot if you can't cram them all in there. Treat that list as helpful guidelines, but don't obsess or your prose will sound stilted and boring.

Using keywords just means using the most basic words about your topic. So when you're writing your copy or header, think of what words somebody might put into a search engine on the topic you're writing about.

Remember my example about the cat that can flush the toilet? Here are two possible headlines:

#1 My Cat Hortense is a Genius

#2 Can Your Cat Learn to Flush the Toilet?"

We know a person looking for information on cat hygiene is more likely to type "cat flush toilet" into Google than "Hortense" and "genius."

If you want somebody to read your piece about how Hortense learned to flush the toilet, leading you to believe there was a poltergeist in the bathroom of your new apartment, use a header that the Googler might think up if she had an interest in toilet-flushing cats.

Instead of learning a bunch of complicated tech stuff, just use imagination and empathy to figure out what somebody might search for if they wanted to read a blogpost like yours.

16—Publishing Your First Post

As I suggested earlier, you should probably compose several blogposts and have them ready to go before you launch that blog. (More if you're planning to jumpstart with more frequent blogging at the beginning.)

You want to give yourself time to avoid the fate of most would-be bloggers, who post once or twice, then leave the deceased blog floating around in cyberspace as a permanent blemish on their brand.

So try to get into a rhythm of posting on a schedule from the get-go.

If you have four or five posts lined up, you'll give yourself a running start.

I personally write a post in Word, save it in my documents, and then copy and paste into the blog. This is because there's auto-save in Word. WordPress has none and Blogger's auto-save is really slow. I learned that the hard way.

But if you use Blogger, I should make it clear that composing in Blogger is the easiest way to post. That's because if you compose in Word and paste into Blogger, you'll have to turn off the "smart quotes" (the curly ones) in Word for that document. It's not that a post won't go live with smart quotes, but the code for smart quotes interferes with the Feedburner RSS feed.

I'm not techy enough to tell you why, but the Feedburner elves can only read stupid quotes. My posts didn't go out for months before I learned that little tidbit of tech info.

So, okay, you've got your standby posts written. They're proofed and ready to go.

Now you want to upload and format the post for the blog.

***

Before You Post
Check Formatting
If you're using WordPress, Word documents paste in fairly intact, except the spacing may be different. If you need to clear any formatting, hit the icon on the tool bar that looks like a little piece of chalk.

In Blogger, the formatting from Word doesn't always come through. I've found the best thing to do is clear your formatting and redo it in the Blogger window. You clear it by selecting the text and hitting the button in the upper right corner that looks like a "T" with a little "x" on the tail.

Upload Images
You've checked and made sure they're out of copyright, haven't you? Then you hit that icon for upload pictures or "add media." Don't forget to give credit, and describe the image in the "alt attributes" window.

Check for SEO
Make sure you put your keyword (s) in your title and in the opening sentence. Then mention it several times (without being tedious and sounding moronic.) You also want a keyword in at least one sub-header and that "alt attributes" window if you're using WordPress.

Select "Tags" or "Labels"
So what are tags? They're like a keyword, but more specific. Their primary purpose is to help index your blog content. While keywords help search engines find your post, tags help people find topics within your blog.

You'll find a spot to put in tags (called "labels" in Blogger) to the right of your "compose post" window. Put a comma between each one.

Say you're writing a blogpost on funny cat tricks. "Funny Cat Tricks" is your keyword. Maybe you're writing about how your cat Hortense taught herself to flush the toilet. You can put in tags like "Hortense," "Cat flushes toilet," "cat hygiene," and "eliminate cat box odor."

If your post mentions your book, *Love is a Cat from Hell* you want to put that as a tag too.

Before you hit "publish" on the post, make sure you've put as many useful tags as you can. (Blogger gives you ten.) Include those keywords and phrases, plus the names of people you're quoting or writing about.

If they're tagged, those people may get a Google Alert that you've mentioned them. That means they may grace your blog with their presence, which is what happened to me with Janet Reid, on my fifth blogpost ever.

I had twelve followers, but there was the "Query Shark" herself, telling me I had a "nicely written post." Oh, how I basked! (She rejected my query anyway, alas.)

So remember that even though tags are primarily intended for indexing, they're also noticed by those all-important spiders, so they can help boost your traffic.

Proofread Again

Once you have the post formatted, it will look different. Hit "preview" and give it another once-over. A different font often reveals things you didn't see before. Every blogger has a few typos once in a while, so don't obsess, but people are more likely to stick around if you've taken the time to polish the post.

***

After You Post
Share to Social Media.

Share to all the sites where you have a presence, even if you don't visit them much. Shares are essential to a new blog. This is when you use those handy "share" buttons I told you to install in Chapter #14.

But make sure your share has something enticing to say. When you share to Facebook, you need to add you own text. You don't want to say "my new blogpost is up!" because nobody but your most loyal cricket will care.

And as far as Twitter, remember what I said about writing Tweetable headers? This is where those come in. If they fit, you'll also want to add one or two hashtags to your Tweet. (See Chapter #22 on "Using Hashtags.")

Share to your Facebook pages (both your personal and author pages) and any groups you belong to that allow notices of a new blogpost. (In a group, this will probably be in a specific thread. Otherwise it's considered spam.)

But instead of saying "My new blogpost is up!" when you share to Facebook," say something like, "do you ever wonder if your apartment is haunted? Today on my blog I talk to an author who wrote a book about meeting a ghost in her bathroom at 3:00 A.M..."

A long established blog like ours gets a lot of traffic from search engines, but we sure didn't in the early days. Our traffic came equally from Facebook and Twitter. These days we get quite a bit from Pinterest as well.

It's best to share your post to twitter several times a day, often using different hashtags. This only takes a minute. (But don't let yourself get distracted by too many other Tweets, or you'll fritter away your writing time. I usually just check my "notifications" when I'm doing quick drive-bys.)

On your other social media, share several times a week while you're getting established.

Send to Subscribers

When you're first starting out, you will probably want to use your own private email list of people who want email notices of new posts, because it takes time to get people to subscribe through the blog. I still have one for special friends and people who would prefer not to sign up for our MailChimp subscription.

But make sure that these are people who want the blog and add a little note about how to unsubscribe. Unfortunately, many new bloggers and new writers spam everybody on their email list, which is a very bad idea.

If you send to all contacts instead of a select group of friends who know the blog is coming, you will be in violation of the American CAN-SPAM act. That means you can be fined over $10,000 dollars for *every* email address that sends a complaint.

Yeah. You really don't want that to happen. And it does. It's not an idle threat.

Accept that it will take time to get that email subscription list going and be patient.

Sign up for Google Alerts on Your Blog Title

If you don't have a Google Alert on your name and the titles of your published books, sign up for those too. You want to know who is noticing your blog, so you can connect.

For some reason Google Alerts only catch about 1 in 10 mentions, so if you don't get any alerts, don't think that means nobody is noticing you.

Reply to Comments

We respond to every comment, even when we get hundreds. Is it time consuming? You bet. But it's one of the most important ways we keep people coming back to the blog.

If you've signed up for email notifications, you'll have a notice in your inbox every time you get a comment, so check frequently on the day the post goes up. After that, you can be more leisurely in your responses.

Delete Spam Comments

A new blog has a spam-blocker that hasn't learned all the ins and outs of your following, so some spam that will come through. Spammers are getting cleverer these days and sometimes they may even seem to have read your post.

They will be full of generic praise. "Great post! You cover topic in goodness. I will share to my brother." Then there will be a series of links to real estate sites in Mumbai or a place to buy knock-off watches.

When you've been waiting for comments and one of these comes in, you may think for a moment it's a real comment and somebody likes you, they really like you!

But they don't. They're just using your blog to get backlinks to the Mumbai site. The tell-tale signs are the links and the less than perfect English skills. Not that you should delete everybody who is grammar-challenged, but pay attention. You can usually tell if it's spam.

Make sure you delete and mark it as spam.

Visit Commenters' Blogs

This may seem like overkill, but if you're just starting out, you're not going to have many comments. And clicking through to visit commenter's blogs will pay off big time. This is how you make friends. That's what this is all about, remember?

Once you get a bigger following, this won't be possible, but it's a great way to get a new blog going.

You are now officially blogging. Congratulations!

17—Considering a Popup Subscription Window?

Don't do it.

Yes, I know. If you've hired somebody to design your blog or website they're going to insist you use a popup. That's because popups are a fad in the tech world right now.

Designers will say "Popups increase your subscriptions ten-fold."

But that's simply not true. Not anymore.

Readers hate popups.

Google hates popups.

The whole world hates popups.

Do you want to be hated?

Then don't go there.

Here's what the marketers at 10Twelve Marketing Agency said about popup ads in their April 2017 blogpost "Seriously, Knock it off with the Popup Ads."

"It is an indisputable fact. People hate popup ads. According to research from the Nielsen Norman Group when users were asked how various forms of advertising affected their web experience, 95% of people rated pop-up ads "negatively" or "very negatively."

The argument is "everybody's getting used to them now." That is, we're already boiled frogs, so it's okay to keep boiling us.

But it isn't.

A popup is harming your brand with every potential reader who leaves your site without seeing your content and never returns.

Think about it: you're driving away 95% of the potential readers of your books—in exchange for meaningless numbers.

So What's a Popup?

It's one of those awful light boxes that now block the content of an increasing number of blogs and other websites, demanding you give up your name and email address before you're allowed to visit the site.

Recently I've visited a number of sites that were blocked by 3, 4, and up to 7 popups. You close one, and there's another...and another...and another.

No content for you!

How can anybody be so ashamed of their own work that they'd block it with 7 popups? Maybe they think that, like Seinfeld's "Soup Nazi," they'll develop a following through reverse psychology.

But personally, I can't get out of those sites fast enough. (Well, I did stay at the one with 7 popups just to see how many I could figure out how to close. I gave up at 7. For all I know the guy may have 10 million popups and no content at all. Nobody will ever know...or care.)

I wanted to tell the guy to find another line of work. If you can't write, don't. But don't pretend to have content and then block it.

The Dreaded Un-Blockable Popup

The man who invented the first popup in the late 1990s, Ethan Zuckerman, has even apologized for "creating one of the most hated tools in the advertiser's toolkit."

By 2004, when the Web was plagued by popup ads, popup blockers became a thing. For a while, the popup nearly disappeared.

But then somebody invented a new kind of popup that can't be blocked. That's because it is technically part of the page, not a different page with a different code. And the dreaded popup was b a-a-a-ck.

That's why the subscription popups that are the scourge of the Internet right now can't be blocked with a popup blocker. They are not technically "popups."

They are official "popup light boxes," also known as "interstitials."

Interstitials do the same thing as the old fashioned despised popup advertisement: they block your content and send potential readers away from your site unless they accept that they are your minions and must do your bidding. These days most popups demand you subscribe to a blog or newsletter and a barrage of daily emails.

Some of those emails are the new toxic kind that says "I see you just visited my site and didn't buy my book. I'm spying on you and I'll bully you until you do."

Yeah. I immediately unsubscribed.

Popups are Getting Meaner.

Many can't be closed until you click on a button that says something like "I'm a moron and I never want to educate myself about this subject."

Some can't be closed unless you sign up for a credit card. Even if you already have their credit card. (The companies who pay for this nonsense tech should hire an accountant who understands the words "bottom line.")

Others grab you as you're trying to escape and tell you you'll never be a success if you leave this website. Some even have a loud, creepy voice-over that calls you a loser for clicking away. So nice to get when the baby is sleeping or you're on a break at work!

Popups are a tool for bullying, pure and simple. They say, "I can waste your time, because I'm more important than you."

Do you respond positively to that message?

Me neither.

Successful Retailers don't use Popups.

Amazon doesn't use popups.

They invented one-click shopping. If you want to beat the competition, you make it easier for people to buy stuff, not harder.

What a concept, right?

And yet these awful things continue to proliferate, like Tribbles on the *Enterprise*.

It's not just that popups irritate people. They are seriously limiting your traffic.

Here's why:

1) Google Downgrades a Site with a Popup.

Popups are annoying on a computer, but on a phone or tablet, they are deadly. They block all the content of a site and often can't be closed.

Google only wants to send people to valid sites, not blocked ones, so if you have a popup that makes your site unreadable on a phone, you get bumped off the SERP. They started doing this in January of 2017.

2) A Popup Drives Away more Readers than People Realize

As the lawyer who blogs at "The Passive Voice" said recently about popups: "When someone arrives at a website they haven't visited before... he/she will form an opinion about that website, including whether they want to visit again, within a few seconds. If those few seconds are a bad experience, they're gone."

Here are some quotes from a recent Facebook thread on the subject, on author Roz Morris's Facebook page.

"Popups are the spawn of Satan."

"So many sites have lost me as a potential customer because they want my email before I can even browse their site."

"There should be a ban on popups. I kind of never sign up to one if they put a popup on the site, out of principle. Get out of my face popups!"

"I've never responded to a popup and close them straight away."

Not one person in the long thread defended them.

3) A Popup Subscription Window Insults Subscribers.

As author Roz Morris said "I don't mind being asked to subscribe, but once I have, you don't have to keep asking me."

I have unsubscribed from blogs where I've been a loyal subscriber for years when they installed a popup.

I wanted to quote them an old Girl Scout song I learned in my childhood.

"Make new friends, but keep the old.
One is silver, but the other is gold."

In trying to get that handful of silver, you're driving away pots of gold.

There is apparently a way to make sure a popup is suppressed when somebody clicks through from your blog notice or newsletter, but it's more complicated and time consuming for the coder, so most people don't bother.

4) Most of the "Conversions" are Meaningless Numbers.

People put the dreaded popups on their websites because they've seen stat numbers that tell them popups result in "conversions." (That's the jargon word for sign-ups.)

But those "converted" people are not subscribing because they want to read your content. They are subscribing to make the popup go away.

Here's what one marketer says: "They click on the popup or put in an email address not because they are interested or wish to subscribe, but because they want the popup to go away and that seems like the easiest way to make it happen."

And a lot of people like me have figured a way around the popup that works fine. When I'm forced to put in an email address in order to see somebody's content I really want to see, I put in a silly fake address, like alreadysubscribed @hotmail or effU@popupssuck. com or something a whole lot ruder.

Yes — they bullied me into giving an email address. Yay! It just doesn't happen to be anybody's actual working address.

But these guys don't care. Because all they want is numbers. Hey, he has 10 million Twitter followers he bought from Lapu-Lapu City just last week! That means he's really special!

But only if he's playing a meaningless numbers game with other meaningless numbers gamers.

If he's an author looking for readers, he's got nothing. Less than nothing. He's got a lot of annoyed visitors who aren't coming back.

Except, of course, for the people who dumped his email advertising into spam. Which leads me to the next point...

5) Your Email Address Can be Flagged as Spam.

Faux "subscribers" who have been bullied into giving up their email address may take the time to unsubscribe, but more often, they'll just hit the spam icon.

If enough people do this, the author can get his own email address permanently marked as spam. His site may even get blocked by McAfee as "dangerous." I know an excellent marketing expert who has fallen for the siren call of multiple popups, and WordPress won't let me link to her site because it is marked "dangerous" by anti-virus software.

And it's not just newsletters. ALL email from an IP address that's been flagged as spam can be blocked.

Web designer Pat Barnes says, "Quality over quantity should be the rule for newsletter subscribers. If people don't read your newsletter, or mark it as spam, then 'deliverability' of all your email is harmed."

6) People Can't Subscribe if They Like Your Content

They couldn't read your content without closing the popup. But now they've read your content and liked it, there's no subscription window.

People who actually WANT subscribers put their signup badge in the upper right hand corner of the sidebar, which is the most prominent spot on the page. It sits there quietly, all the time, so it's there when the READER wants it, not when you happen to feel like hitting them in the face with it.

***

I let an "expert" talk me into putting a popup on our blog when we tried our ill-advised experiment in monetizing. It lasted about a week until we got so many complaints I got rid of it.

Yes, we got a lot of "conversions." But the next week, we got a whole lot of unsubscribes. Almost identical numbers. Hmmm.

If you write good content, why not let people read it and then decide if they want more? If you write bad content, no amount of blocking and bullying will get people to come back, no matter what the numbers-manipulators say.

So skip the popup and make friends instead of enemies.

18—Blog or Newsletter?

Everybody's probably been telling you to start an email newsletter. "The writer with the biggest email list wins" is the current mantra of pretty much every book marketer in the industry. The author newsletter is supposed to be the most important weapon in your book marketing arsenal.

But a blog has email subscribers too. And I think a blog is more effective. If you don't have a newsletter, I'd suggest you start with a blog and put the newsletter on hold until you know if you need one.

When new posts go up on Sunday, our blog subscribers get a notice in their email inbox.

But we don't use the list of subscribers for anything else. Certainly not advertising.

Author newsletters usually fit into four categories:

1) A simple notice of book launches and freebie or sale runs.

2) An old school, chatty note that reads like the newsy Christmas letter you get from Aunt Susie. Pictures of the author on vacation and news about her life and family.

3) The "street team" newsletter, where readers are treated as members of a team whose duty it is to review and promote the author's work.

4) The hard-sell advertising email that aims at getting new customers.

I have no problem with #1. If I wrote more quickly, I

might have one too.

But the others, not so much, it's mostly a Golden Rule thing. I don't spam unto others what I don't want spammed unto me.

I know many authors who feel the same way. Catherine Ryan Hyde mentioned her dislike of newsletters in the Foreword. She has sold well over a million books on Amazon in the past couple of years without a newsletter.

On her website, Catherine says:

"For years I've been encouraged to keep an email list of readers, but I have always refused. I feel that emailing you to tell you I have a new book out is spamming you. So, though you give me your email address for the purpose of giveaways, I don't save those addresses or use them for any other purpose. I put news on my website, on this blog, and on my social media pages, so you know where to find it. If you want it. That's the key."

It's no wonder she's the person who brought the expression "Pay it Forward" into our culture.

Unwanted Newsletters Can Get You in Trouble.

Sending newsletters to people who haven't subscribed (by taking addresses from your Facebook friends or Twitter followers or buying email lists) is a bad idea.

It's not just unethical and annoying. It's also against that CAN-SPAM Act I talked about in Chapter #16.

I realize authors don't think of their newsletters as spam, but the law may. It defines spam as "any electronic mail message the primary purpose of which is the commercial advertisement or promotion of a commercial product or service."

The law requires you to have an unsubscribe function that's easily seen and is simple to use. Light gray letters in a flyspeck font don't cut it. And you have to honor an unsubscribe request within 10 business days: "once people have told you they don't want to receive more messages from you, you can't sell or transfer their email addresses, even in the form of a mailing list."

There are additional fines if you have harvested the email address without the recipient's permission (or bought it from a Russian hacker.)

Don't risk it.

You May be Flagged as a Spammer.

As I've said, when people get unwanted email, they'll likely send it to the spam folder. Google has a pretty good memory, and when you mark something as spam in Gmail, Google remembers. When something is sent into spam by enough people, Google will helpfully do it for us.

This means that email address will be marked as spam forever. Even people who actually want your author newsletter won't be able to get it unless they fish it out of their spam folder.

BTW, this is also a reason not to mass-query agents and bloggers. Mass emails usually get sent to spam. Your query is reaching nobody and you're marking yourself as a spammer. Unless you do your homework and address each agent or blogger individually, you are not only wasting your time, but destroying your own reputation.

Here are the reasons I prefer a blog with a subscription signup feature rather than an author newsletter.

A blog:

1) Attracts new readers.

An author newsletter only goes to existing customers who have asked to get it. (If you're doing it legally.) These are generally people who have already bought your book.

So unless you're one of those speedy writers who can pop a book out every month, you're directing your sales pitch at precisely the people who are guaranteed not to buy: the ones who already have what you're selling.

But a blog is out there in public on the Web. Any new reader can stumble on it and learn about your book and maybe even buy one.

2) Is interactive.

A lively comment section is often a blog's biggest appeal. If you respond to comments (which I strongly recommend,) you can answer questions and expand on the information in the post.

An author newsletter is broadcast to a limited audience. There can't be any discussion, except one-to-one.

Your reader can't ask questions about your content unless they email you back. Yes, of course you can start an email conversation with every reader individually, but nobody will see your answer but that one reader.

And the process is a huge waste of your time compared to open conversation on a blog that everybody can see (including Google) and everybody can join in.

3) Gets Google's attention.

Something you put in a newsletter stays in the newsletter. Search engines will never know about it. Your writing will be a secret locked up in a closed environment.

Some of the biggest breaks in my career have come from simple Google searches that picked up my blog posts. When an editor at *More* magazine was researching an article on "Bag Lady Syndrome," she Googled it. The third entry on the SERP was a guest post I wrote about women and homelessness when promoting *No Place Like Home*. She immediately contacted me for an interview.

As a result, I got a featured spot in a major New York glossy magazine that targets my demographic, older educated women—and it was absolutely free. Advertising there would have cost me thousands.

If I'd written the piece in a newsletter, that never would have happened—nor would any of the other publicity I've received when people contact me because my blog posts come up in a Google search. It happens quite often.

It's free marketing. Why give that up?

4) Can be shared.

I'm always disappointed when I read something great in a newsletter and realize I can't share it with my Twitter followers or Facebook peeps. Sometimes I even go to the trouble of visiting the author's website to see if the article is there.

It almost never is. So your piece—and the advertising attached—is forever sealed into a handful of inboxes instead of being spread around the Web. Unless you have a paid newsletter with premium content, this does little for your bottom line.

5) Reaches new subscribers.

How are subscribers going to find you? On your website? Websites don't get much traffic unless they have an active blog attached. Are you going to blog regularly *and* send out a weekly newsletter?

I realize why some authors are resorting to buying mailing lists. It's miserable trying to get readers to your website if you don't have good, fresh content to draw them. And if they're not at your website, they aren't going to see your subscription signup even if you have the most obnoxious pop-up in the world.

Authors do get signups through contests or giveaways on their Facebook author pages and that can work, but those campaigns cost money, and as I mentioned before, people often unsubscribe immediately after getting the bribe.

So you might consider a blog instead of an expensive newsletter for keeping your readers "in the loop" between books. Aggressive business bloggers have given blogs a bad name, but they're solid workhorses that can advance your career much better than the currently more stylish newsletter.

19—The Author-Blogger's Secret Weapon: Google Plus

Okay, I know you're all groaning. Google Plus? It's history!

Yup. I expected it to last a little longer and I was wrong. I figured Google could afford to keep it going even though it was never the place where the cool kids hung out. It was always more like LinkedIn—a business tool rather than a place to chat and share funny cat pictures and videos.

But when I wrote this book in 2017, Google Plus was the fastest way to get your new blogposts noticed by the Google search engine. So I recommended it strongly.

What I didn't know was that it was a magnet for hackers. In 2018, after a second massive hack of Google Plus, Alphabet, the parent company of Google, decided to kill off the clunky, unpopular social media platform for good.

After years of ill-conceived updates and ever-falling user numbers, Google Plus shuffled off its mortal coil on April 2, 2019.

Any links to your Google Plus profile will bring up the dreaded 404 Not Found page, so make sure you don't have any of the old links on your blog. They are now broken links that will get angry responses from your readers.

People who were still using Google Groups have mostly moved to Facebook or one of the new Facebook alternatives like MeWe.

The "G+" share button should have disappeared from your blog, but if it's still there, you can remove it by going to your dashboard and clicking on "sharing" then "sharing buttons" then "edit sharing buttons."

This is a reminder of how fast the online world changes. When I first started blogging, MySpace was where you got noticed and writers congregated at RedRoom.

But you know what's still around? Blogging. I'm not so sure the Blogger platform will be around forever though, so if you have a Blogger blog, make sure you're backing up your work regularly.

If you're just starting a blog now, I think WordPress is the safest place to be. Since Blogger is owned by Google, and Google has shown it has no trouble pulling the plug on its less popular platforms, Blogger could be next to go.

But this also shows how great it is to have a blog rather than a static website. On a blog, old information and broken links can be repaired in minutes, and you don't have to go through all the hassle of paying a web designer to change the text every time there's a big change like this.

20—A Blog Can Change and Grow with Your Career

Yes, I know a writer starting a blog right now faces some problems:

1) There are already a trillion writers out there lecturing the blogosphere about how to write vivid characters, prop up saggy middles and avoid adverbs. A lot of them probably know more than you.

2) If you're a writer with books to sell, you want to reach a general audience, not just other writers selling books.

So how can you be different? How do you create a blog that somebody will read—somebody besides your stalker ex-boyfriend and your mom?

The most important thing to remember with any kind of blog is you need to offer something fresh, informative, and/or entertaining.

How you approach your blog is going to depend a whole lot on your stage in the publishing process and your immediate goals.

Stage #1: When You're a Developing Writer.

You're working on your first or second novel, and maybe have a few stories in literary journals or a couple of contest wins. You want to be a published author sometime soon, but you're not quite ready to focus on writing as a career.

Your goal: LEARNING THE PUBLISHING BUSINESS AND NETWORKING.

You want to make friends in the writing community for career help and mutual support. You want to learn the best writing techniques, network with publishing professionals, and educate yourself about the business.

If you're in stage #1, it's okay to blog about writing. I know most blog gurus tell you not to do this, but I think that caveat is aimed more at people at stage #2 and #3.

I'm not talking about lecturing on craft as if you're a pro when you're not. But an equal-to-equal post about some interesting trick you've discovered about writing the dreaded synopsis, or what agents are looking for this month is just fine when you're reaching out to other writers.

Why do you want to reach other writers? Because networking with other writers is essential in today's market. Joint promotions and anthologies and boxed sets will be some of your most powerful marketing strategies once you're published. The friends you make now will be a huge asset to you later on in your career.

Plus I know a number of authors who got their agents through a referral from a fellow blogger. I found both my publishers through blogging.

Also, I'm not sure I would have made it through the darkest rejection phases if it hadn't been for the support of writer blog friends.

When you have a writing blog, you get to participate in blog hops, flash fiction swaps, contests — and all kinds of networking events that help you meet people who can be important in your future career.

Stage #2: When You're Entering the Marketplace.

You're querying agents or getting ready to self-publish. You've got a couple of books polished and ready to go. You have a business plan.

You've been to writing conferences, taken classes, and hired a freelance editor if you're going indie. Your writing is at a professional level.

Your goal: BUILDING PLATFORM

You want to get your name out there to the general public. When you query an agent or ask for a blurb or review, you want a Google search to bring you up on the first page.

If you're a stage #2 writer, you should heed the blog guru advice not to blog about writing. You've got a trillion competitors. (Yes, I blog about writing, but I started a long time ago, and I already had an audience from my writing column at *Inkwell Newswatch*.)

So try something that's related to your writing but has a unique slant. But don't restrict yourself too much. Leave room to grow and change. You may not even know yet what kind of people will be interested in your work.

This is a time when links will really help build your platform.

Focus on your genre or subgenre. Discuss movies, videogames, TV shows, even jewelry and costumes—as long as they relate to your books—and link to other sites that discuss them.

It's a good time to blog about your hometown or state, especially if they're the setting of your novels. Link to local landmarks and the Chamber of Commerce.

Offer links to important information. If you're writing a memoir or fiction about certain health issues, promote organizations that help with those issues. Link to support groups and they might even link back.

Provide people with the benefit of your research. If you're writing historical fiction about a certain time period— post the research on your blog. (This is doubly useful because it will help keep you from cramming it all into the novel at the expense of story.) Have to research guns for a thriller? Poisons for a cozy? Are you basing the story on a real case? There are people who would love to read about this stuff.

This is also a good time to appeal to another Internet community. If that historical novel is based on a real person or your own family history, you could target readers from the genealogy blogosphere and links to historical research sites. If your heroine loves to fish, sew, or collect stuff, connect with blogs for fly fisherpersons, quilters, or collectors of floaty pens.

You might offer a forum for people in your target demographic. If you write for a particular group — single urban women, Boomers, stay-at-home moms, or the just-out-of-college dazed and confused — focus on their issues and link to sites of interest to them.

Your focus during this stage should be spreading a wide net and getting yourself on the radar of as many people as possible.

Stage #3: For the Published Author

Your agent/marketing dept. says, "Get thee to the blogosphere!"

Or you realize the brilliantly-blurbed *oeuvre* you've self-published is sitting there on Amazon with only two sales in three months — both to your mom — because nobody has heard of it — or you.

Your goal: FINDING AND CONNECTING WITH READERS

If you've reached Stage #3, you can be more eclectic. People will be coming to your blog because they want to get to know you and find out more about your books — so focusing on one subject isn't as important.

The blog becomes a place to showcase who you are, like a magazine or newspaper column. It's not a place to toot your own horn as much as share things of interest to you that will also be of value to your readers.

So you can continue whatever you've been doing in Stage #1 and #2, plus add stuff about you and your books.

Yes, you can talk about your books. I think people are silly who say you shouldn't use your blog for self-promotion. That's why you're in the blogosphere in the first place. It's fine as long as you don't use hard-sell tactics and make sure you provide something besides "buy my book!"

Each type of blog can evolve into another as your goals change.

21—Blog Hops and Blog Tours

I've mentioned blog "hops" and "tours" several times in this book. So what are they?

A BLOG HOP is a multi-blogger event where a group of bloggers band together—usually to write on a particular theme. They visit and comment on each other's blogposts on that theme. They often offer readers some sort of incentive to go to their blogs and read their work.

There is one central site where the participating authors are listed and readers can click through to the various blogs to enter giveaways or read samples of the authors' work. Blog hops can take various formats. Some hops are for a limited time and authors offer perks and giveaways to readers who visit the site and leave a comment or sign up on a list.

It's usually organized by one blogger who will provide the central site or blog where the participants and their links are listed. The blog-hoppers then click through to all the participating blogs, "follow" each other, and leave comments.

Often the blog hop creator will give you a badge to put in your sidebar that identifies you as a member of the hop.

It can be time-consuming and it will eat into your writing time, so I don't recommend doing this often, but if you have a chance to join one, it can really pay off in back-links and a big jump in the traffic to your blog.

Plus it's a great way to meet other authors. This can lead to getting together to publish an anthology or a boxed set.

Multi-author anthologies and boxed sets are a fantastic way to increase book sales. It sure worked for me. I've participated in seven anthologies and two boxed sets and they all brought a measurable increase in my sales.

In the monetized blog community, blog hop organizers sometimes charge a fee for participating. But I don't recommend joining a fee-charging blog hop. That will get you out of the author blog community and it probably won't pay off.

The benefits of a blog hop are:
- More traffic to your blog
- Exposure to new readers
- Networking opportunities

The Standard Rules of a Blog Hop:

1) "Follow" the hosts and your fellow hoppers.

2) If there is one, put the Blog Hop badge on your sidebar.

3) Post on the designated theme at designated intervals. Sometimes this involves blogging every day for the duration of the hop. Way too grueling for me, but some bloggers manage to do it. Like NaNoWriMo (National Novel Writing Month) this can be an intense bonding experience if you're up to it.

4) Visit as many of the other participants' blogs and read what they've written on the theme and leave comments

***

A BLOG TOUR is a week to month long event when an author visits a series of book and author blogs to guest post and give interviews (and hopefully get some reviews) usually to promote a book launch.

A blog tour is like an old fashioned book tour, but instead of visiting bookstores and libraries all over the country, you visit blogs. (And can wear your sweats and bunny slippers.)

Paid blog tours are waning in popularity, but you can still get an arranged, paid blog tour from numerous agencies. Make sure they are vetted and recommended by somebody you trust. At the height of their popularity, some unscrupulous blog tour operators abused both the bloggers and the authors and things got unpleasant.

Most of the book bloggers aren't paid, but the author may be paying a lot, so she might start ordering the blogger around as if she's a paid employee, and bad feelings ensue.

It's best if you can arrange your own blog tour, which you can do if you have your own blog and have been getting out in the blogosphere to meet other author-bloggers and reviewers in your genre.

But blog tours can be a lot of work. And sometimes, especially for first-time self-published authors, blog tours don't generate as many sales as anticipated.

There are specific steps you can take to help make your blog tour more successful.

1) Get to Know Book Bloggers in Your Genre.

If you already have established relationships with other bloggers, and know how to interact with comments, you're way ahead of the game.

If you know what that blogger's audience is like, you can tailor your post to them and that can pay off big time. When I did my first blog tour, which I arranged myself, I visited one blog with a smallish following, but I knew they were mostly well-read older women, so I pitched aspects of my story that would appeal to them and made a huge number of sales that day.

2) Know Your Genre.

Book marketing is a genre-based business. You need to network inside your genre. If your book is mainstream, or a hybrid like my rom-com mysteries, it can still be worthwhile if you stick to bloggers in one genre.

My first blog tour I went to mostly women's fiction and chick lit blogs. For the second, I focused on mystery readers. I found the women's fiction readers bought more books. Maybe because there isn't such a glut in the genre.

3) Offer Quality Content.

Don't just blurb your book. Offer something inspirational about what sparked the story or something personal about yourself that's funny or entertaining

You can also offer a kind of "reader's guide" of the kind you might give a book group. That can bring in comments about your theme and setting.

You also want to send good images: a .jpg of your book cover, author photo and anything else that might illustrate your piece.

***

Blog hops and blog tours may be going out of fashion these days, but they still can give you a lot of exposure and help you and your book with visibility.

22—Using Hashtags to Boost Your Blog Traffic

Most social networks use hashtags (the # symbol that used to be called "the pound sign" in the US.) If you put the # symbol in front of a word—without a space in between—that makes the word "live." You can tell it's working when the word changes color. That will make your post appear when people search for that topic.

They can really increase your blog traffic from Twitter and Instagram. LinkedIn doesn't use them, and although Facebook has had them since 2013, they don't show up very often. They're handy if you're looking for a particular topic, but not necessary. Pinterest used to discourage them but accepts them now.

Here's how they work: if you put #amediting on the link to your post about "How to Self-Edit Your Short Fiction," and somebody puts "#amediting" in the Twitter search window, they can find your post.

Some Popular Twitter Writing Hashtags.

These are great for networking with other writers. But if you're writing about travel, or history, costumes, or whatever, put some possible hashtags in Twitter and see what comes up. Use the most popular ones.

You can also search for hashtags on a site called TagDef (short for "tag definition.") It's especially helpful if you see a lot of posts in your subject with a certain tag and want to know what it means. Say you see a lot of writing posts are tagged with #myWANA, you can look it up on TagDef and see it means "We Are Not Alone" — the name of Kristen Lamb's writing support community. (I highly recommend WANA for new writers.)

All hashtags are hyperlinked so when you click on a hashtag, you'll navigate to a page filled with Tweets that carry that hashtag.

For a hashtag to work, you can't separate the words or add other letters or symbols. For example, #amwriting! wouldn't work because adding the exclamation mark changes it.

Here's a partial list of writing hashtags:

#1LineWednesday: share the best line from one of your books on Wednesdays and use this hashtag.

#99c: Looking for a new ebook? Put this tag in the Twitter search bar for a list of cheap and discounted books. And it's great when you're running a sale yourself. Also use #KindleBargain and #Countdown if you're running a sale.

#Amazon / #GooglePlay / #Kobo / #iTunes / #Smashw ords: let your readers know where your book is available.

#amwriting / #amediting: advice or questions for writers going through the same process.

#AuthorChat: for networking with other authors.

#askagent: for authors seeking representation. You can also find out what the publishing industry is looking for right now.

#askeditor: for editing questions.

#bibliophile / #bookworm / #reader: add when you're posting about your book.

#bookmarket / #bookmarketing / #GetPublished / #pubtip: I use these a lot for info about marketing.

#eBook: good for when you have a new one to promote. Best to only use when you have a sale or promo. Twitter is littered with #ebook spam.

#FollowFriday / #FF: This is a long-timeTwitter tradition for thanking your Retweeters by giving them exposure to a wider audience. Use sparingly. This tradition has kind of passed its sell-by date, but some people still do it. It's best if you only thank two or three people though. Anything that's just a bunch of hashtags or Twitter handles tends to get ignored.

#bookgiveaway / #Free / #Giveaway / #FreeDownload / #FreebieFriday. If you've got a book giveaway promo, these will let people know. The latter is for sharing on Fridays, obviously.

#Greatreads / #FridayRead: These are for sharing what you're reading, not for promoting your own book. But it's a great way to network with people who read your genre.

#KidLit / #PictureBook / #Crimefiction / #Suspense / #Mystery / #Erotica / #Paranormal / #DarkThriller / #Dark Fantasy / #memoir, etc., really help when you're promoting a genre book. Readers will look specifically for them.

#writegoal: This is what you use when you want to announce how many words you hope to write that day. I find it really tedious, but if numbers motivate you, it might connect you with other writers who feel the same.

#WriterWednesday / #WW: Again, this one is kind of over, but you can use it on Wednesdays to recommend authors you admire.

#WritersBlock / #WriteMotivation: use these when you're in need of a little inspiration, or have some to share.

#WritersLife: use this for a funny quote about writing or the writing process. Also useful for blogposts on the subject.

#writetip / #writingtip: if you don't have time to take a workshop, try using these hashtags to learn more about craft.

You'll probably find a few hashtags will work great for you and others won't reach anybody who's interested in your blog. But playing around with them may get you a lot more blog traffic.

A word of warning: don't overdo hashtags! They're hard to read and make your text look silly. You'll see some hard-sell types whose entire Twitter profile is made up of hashtags. I never follow those people back. Two or three hashtags per Tweet, profile, or post is the polite limit.

23—Guest Blogging: A Powerful, Free Marketing Tool

Not all writers are cut out to have a blog. Author blogs don't just take time, commitment, and discipline—they require the ability to switch gears from your WIP to blogging on a regular basis. If you're working on a novel, this can be a major shift.

But guest blogging allows you to take advantage of blogs even if you don't want to go through the hassles of maintaining your own site.

Visiting blogs by writing a guest post is a fantastic way to improve visibility and sell your books. And it doesn't cost a thing.

It's useful for everybody from new writers who haven't built much of a platform yet—to long-time pros who want to promote a new title or build their mailing list.

Most host bloggers will allow you to link to your website and to your book "buy" pages, so the post can both improve your name recognition and sell books. It's free advertising and boosts your search engine rank. You can also offer giveaways as promos or an incentive to sign up for your list.

Some authors don't have blogs and manage to do very well by simply guesting on other blogs several times a month. Ruth Harris did that before I talked her into joining me as a permanent guest.

You don't have to be a published author to benefit from

guesting on blogs. Guest blogging before you have a book out is a fantastic way to pave the way for a launch and get name recognition, and it's also an excellent way to raise your profile if you're a freelancer.

But don't assume all bloggers will welcome you. The higher ranked the blog, the more guest blog queries they're getting — and they may be burned out on the whole process.

On our blog we get twenty or more queries a week, which makes me sad, because we have to turn away most of them. We host only a dozen guests per year and book many months in advance. With only 4 posts a month, each post has to offer something pretty special to keep those numbers where they are.

We don't often find the experts we need in "cold" email queries.

Unfortunately, the one thing most requests have in common is they show the writer hasn't visited the blog. (Although they always give it high, generic praise.) But they usually don't have the slightest idea what the blog is about or who our readers are.

Sometimes they offer content — absolutely FREE! — written about "the subject of your choice" and the only thing they seem to know about us is that we've got a big readership.

Most queriers don't have a clue that we have a non-monetized blog focused on the publishing industry, so they pitch something totally irrelevant.

I usually answer each query individually (which makes me feel a lot of empathy with agents and editors.) I thank the writers and wish them all the best in their careers and then suggest that they, um, read a blog before querying.

After a morning in the guest-blog-request trenches, I decided to do some research. I discovered guest blogging is one of the most popular ways to raise SEO and get backlinks to websites.

Unfortunately, it has also become a preferred venue for

dodgy marketers and spammers. Many will provide mediocre content full of links to websites unrelated to the post — often ads for male enhancement pills and "adult" sites.

Yeah, I felt kinda dumb when I realized I'd been working so hard to spare the feelings of porn spammers.

But not every potential guest is offering spammy content. Many queries come from editing professionals, designers, and fellow authors who have something worthwhile to share.

Trouble is, they usually approach in an impersonal way and, although they may reference one post, they don't have a feel for our tone or content. Often they make demands but don't offer much in return. Yes, we know it will help your book launch to get your covers and links in front of our readers, but if your post is simply a thinly disguised ad for your book or services, we could lose the readership we've worked so hard to build.

Also, guest posts seldom get the hits our own posts do (readers seem to view guests like substitute teachers — not really part of the curriculum.) So a guest spot is something of a gift. You need to make bloggers want to turn their own bookselling platform over to you, either because you have a big following of your own, you offer something fresh and unique, or they like you. Preferably all of the above.

Getting your (high quality) work onto a well-known blog is still one of the best ways to promote your brand. The marketers are right about getting those backlinks from the blog to your own website or author page. It's a great way to get the Google spider-bots to notice you and raise your own website or blog higher on a Google search page.

But selling books isn't the same as selling shampoo or refrigerators. With books, you're often better off targeting lesser-known blogs. Forget the SEO and Alexa ratings.

Look for blogs that address your target audience.

Here are some tips for authors who want to try guest blogging:

Research Blogs to Find Where Your Readers Hang Out.

Think about where a guest post might reach the most potential buyers for your books. Where are your readers likely to be? Be creative. Consider your genre, setting, and your protagonist's hobbies or quirks.

Write romance? You'll reach a lot more writers at "Romance University" or "Romance Divas" than my blog, which is for writers of all genres.

But you might reach even more romance readers if you guest at a blog that's not for writers at all. If your romances are set in a particular place, consider reaching out to travel blogs about the area of your setting. People planning vacations buy more fiction than people arguing about prologues. Do a search on your setting and start clicking.

Consider group blogs of authors in your genre. Write mysteries? Blogs like "Jungle Red Writers," "Deadly Divas," or "Hey there's a Dead Guy in the Living Room" are great places to query for a guest spot. Google "mystery blogs" and you'll be amazed at how many are out there.

Maybe your sleuth is a real estate agent. (There seems to be a growing subgenre of real estate mysteries. I think it deserves its own category. They're lots of fun.) What if you could be a guest blogger for a real estate site? You could make sales to people who'd never buy a mystery otherwise. That's pure gold. Try a pitch to an in-house blog for a real estate network about a particular problem your sleuth runs up against.

Have a protagonist who's caring for an aging parent? Try reaching out to caregiver blogs. Have a military memoir? Try a blog about military collectibles or recent military history.

Google your subject matter and read some of the blogs that come up.

Don't wait until your book is finished. Reading those blogs can be a great source of information and inspiration for your story, too.

Visiting non-writing blogs is also a great way to ask for reviews. There will be no conflict with Amazon's murky rules that exclude some authors from writing book reviews.

Google is your friend. You can pretty much find a blog on any subject you can name. Blogs are one of the best resources for writers both for research and finding readers...and they're FREE!

Read Several Posts before you Query, Including Comments.

Seems like a no-brainer, but if you visit the blog, you're already ahead of 90% of the guest blog wannabes who query.

There are actually blog gurus who tell guest blog wannabes not to visit a blog before querying. They say using a generic template saves time. Apparently getting 1000 rejections and no guest post gigs (and some enemies) isn't a waste of time.

I'm amazed at how much bad advice is out there about blogging.

But use your own personal brain. Aren't you more likely to respond positively to somebody who shows respect and intelligence than a lying moron? Me, too. And I think we're not alone.

So I'm telling you to visit the blog and read it. Not just one post. Read several—and make sure you check the comments. That's how you can tell if the audience is right for the topic you're pitching. You don't want to pitch a "how to send your first query letter" article to an audience of published authors or a technical post on SEO to a poetry circle.

In fact, you can get great ideas for topics to write about by reading what people are asking questions about in the comments.

Leave a Comment.

If bloggers have seen your name before, they're going to pay more attention to your query. The best way to break in is to get to know other bloggers and the blog community.

If you show your expertise in a certain subject in a blog comment, the blogger may even seek you out and ask you to be a guest.

That's how we find most of our guests: in the comment threads.

Note: I'm not talking about posting a query in a comment thread, which is a no-no. But when people write a useful comment that shows expertise and good writing skills, I often ask them to guest post.

It's how I connected with Ruth Harris. She commented several times on my blog and I remembered reading her books when they were topping the bestseller lists. When I saw she had no blog of her own...the rest is history.

Be Real and use a Friendly Tone.

Remember writing for the web means using sub-headers, lists, bullet points, bolding, and lots of white space. Complete sentences are not required. A blogpost is not a news article, college thesis, or tech manual. Offer information in an entertaining, non-condescending way. Keep things light and encouraging.

If you have a tale of woe, make sure the ending is hopeful and upbeat. And be careful of language. Make sure it's appropriate for the blog. Some blogs allow four-letter words and blunt speech, but most do not.

Read. The. Guidelines.

I'm going to repeat that: READ THE GUIDELINES. That would be before you query. "Guidelines" is kind of a misnomer. They are directions. Rules. Commandments. Follow them.

For me, a pitch can be a couple of short sentences, but if a blogger says she wants a four-page, single-spaced pitch, write a four-page, single-spaced pitch.

Almost all bloggers will want you to include a short bio, a head shot, and links to your website, author page, and social media. They may also ask you to include images. (Make sure they are not under copyright.)

Some bloggers may prefer to give you a topic, or may offer questions so the post can be in an interview format. They may have specific requirements for number and size of photos and/or word count. They may suggest you offer a book give-away.

Don't assume you "know the ropes." The blogger is the boss. If you want to get the gig, you have to please the blogger, not me or any other author of a blogging book.

Check out Other Guest Post on the Blog.

If you're a beginning writer, you probably won't land a spot on a blog where bestselling authors and movie stars go to promote their books. You also won't benefit from guesting if the blogger has been lazy and accepts a lot of mediocre content.

Our guests are mostly seasoned authors, award winners, or experts in their fields (and once we really hosted movie star Terence Stamp.) They also need to be good general-interest writers who don't use too much jargon, because tech-speak reads like Klingon to a lot of our readers. (It sure does to me.)

A humorous approach is a big plus.

But you don't have to be a movie star or a bestseller to guest for us. You do need to be experienced in writing solid Web content and have something fresh and unique to say that's of general interest to writers.

The most important thing you can do to get a coveted guest blog spot is individualize your pitch to each specific blog. (Just the way you individualize agent queries.)

On our blog, we don't post personal stories, but lots of blogs do. Most bloggers love success (or failure) stories, interesting anecdotes about researching your book, posts based on your book research, or funny stories about the writing life. A lot of bloggers like interviews, too.

Do Not Spam.

Make sure you're not writing a blatant advertisement for

your book or services. Offer something fresh, not just ad copy.

Offer new, useful, informative content that can't be found everywhere. Cutting and pasting tired information from around the Web—or even your own blog—usually won't cut it.

But note that if you often blog about your special field of expertise, a reblogged post may be fine.

I've often read a great post and asked the blogger to do a version of the piece for us.

Send a Professional Query (via Email.)

As I said above, don't request a guest spot via comment thread. Generally a Tweet or direct message won't work either.

BTW, when I wrote those exact words in a post about guest blogging several years ago, somebody pasted a query into the comments, showing they hadn't understood a word of the post. Not a good advertisement for their language skills.

Write your query with proper paragraphing, punctuation, capitalization, and spelling. That means probably no emojis, unless the blogger also uses them. This is true whether you're asking for a review, interview, spotlight, or guest post spot. Be businesslike, concise, respectful, and don't lie.

Seriously. Don't make stuff up.

A blog query is very similar to an agent query.

• **Open with a mention of why you're querying this particular blogger**. This is where you can show off that you've actually read several posts on the blog. As I said, it will put you head and shoulders above the competition.

• **Pitch your project (s) in a couple of sentences.** You can have one pitch or several. I prefer several, so I can choose. Sometimes a great potential guest may have a wonderful idea, but we're running a post on that subject next week, so I'll want to see what else they've got. Pitches don't have to be elaborate. Just give your possible topics with a few sentences after each about your angle and why you're qualified to write about it. A bulleted list works fine. Give word count if it's not specified in the guidelines. If you're querying the folks at Big Name Real Estate blog to promote your new real estate cozy, Murder in Escrow, you might pitch a topic especially for them: "How to Market a 'Haunted' House—selling a house where there's been a high-profile death."

- **Give your credentials:** Choose a few of the best ones—skip that honorable mention poetry award and the penmanship prize you got in 5th grade. Anything relevant to the post you're pitching is good: "I've been a realtor for nearly twenty years, so I've sold my share of houses where people have died."
- **Link to your best "clips"** in online magazines, your own blog, and other guest posts. If you've been a guest of a big, popular writing blog like The Book Designer, Jane Friedman, Writers on the Storm, Fiction University, Romance University, etc., that's a big plus. And remember a clip is an *example* of your writing. Don't simply offer another blogger a repost of the same material. You can offer to write for them on the same subject, but don't simply offer a cut-and-paste. That's disrespectful to both blogs.
- **If you have a big online following, toot your own horn.** Even if your work isn't published in book form, if you've got a big social media following, that can actually be more attractive to a blogger than a major award or a big bestseller. If you know your blog's Alexa rating and it's under a million, do include that. (That's the Alexa rating system I talked about in Chapter #7, not the Amazon device.)

If this Guest Post is to be Part of a Blog Tour, Mention Specifics.

If you have a time window, giveaways, contests, etc., and you want this post to be part of a blog tour, be sure to tell the blogger. You can say, "*Murder in Escrow* launches in [date] and I'd like a spot in [time window.]"

Make sure you will be available in that time window to

respond to comments. Not all bloggers respond to all comments the way we do, but responding to comments is a great way to make connections and sell books, so if you're not available, you're losing sales.

***

Guest blogging is one of the best ways to build your platform—and it's free advertising for your books. But remember you're asking for a favor.

If you're a new writer without a presence in the blogosphere, it may be worth your while to launch your book with a professional blog tour (See Chapter #21), which will involve guest blogging as well as interviews and reviews. It will cost you some money, but doesn't have to be hugely expensive, and it can do wonders for your visibility.

24—Author Blogging Can be a Stepping Stone to Many Careers

Since I started blogging eight years ago, I've watched a lot of author-bloggers succeed as writers. They may not have had huge success as novelists (although some have). But for all of them, the blog was the first step to a successful career in publishing.

A lot of blogs disappear, of course. Blogging well requires discipline, good 21st century writing skills, and the empathy to understand what your readers want. But if you stick to it, blogging can pay off in major ways.

As I said, author blogs only need to appeal to a target readership, not vast hordes of consumers. They don't generate income directly. Instead they provide a platform for your writing and a way to communicate with readers and fellow writers.

In my own little corner of the blogosphere, I've watched many authors find success through this kind of blogging.

Good stuff often happens when writers take a different path from the one they started on: that Blog—Agent—Book Deal—Fame-and-Fortune path most of us fantasize about when we begin to write.

Early in my blogging career I made friends with a lot of newbie author-bloggers who were all trying to get the attention of agents and publishers. A lot of us were using our blogs to track our journeys to publication, so we visited each other's blogs for industry information and also mutual support and friendship.

Then the Kindle Revolution happened, and I lost track of a lot of my blogger friends as I spent 18-hour days publishing ten books with two digital publishers as well as keeping this blog going.

But recently I've been seeking out some of my old blog-friends. Seeing the paths they've taken has been fascinating. A bunch have disappeared from the blogosphere, but others have used their blogs as stepping stones to great careers—not necessarily the careers they'd planned, but creative, fulfilling ones.

So do think about the paths available to you as you decide whether or not to start a blog (or lament that your blog doesn't seem to be doing much for your writing career.)

Features Writer

One writer who was a helpful source of information about social media didn't land an agent, or even finish her novel.

But she got a paying gig for a magazine as an expert in social media. That led to jobs at other magazines.

Now she's a successful magazine advice columnist with a big following.

I'm sure she's still got that novel in her files, but now she has a professional writing job that doesn't involve agents, rejections, or the hassles of self-publishing.

Other book bloggers have found regular work as reviewers or freelance writers for high-paying magazines.

Blogging is a great way to show off your writing chops no matter what the subject matter.

Literary Agent

At least two of the bloggers I met early on are now successful literary agents. They started with book blogs that specialized in reviews. They became well known for careful, unbiased reviews, and eventually were approached by agents looking for interns.

After an apprenticeship, both became full-time agents. One has recently opened her own agency.

All from a little blog.

Editor of a Literary Journal or Magazine

I have at least three friends who have been invited to edit new online journals or literary magazines because the founder of the journal or company that owned the magazine admired their blogs.

If you write and curate good content, people notice.

Content Provider

We learn by doing. Writing on your own blog teaches you what works and what doesn't when writing for the Web. There are lucrative careers writing content for websites and blogs.

Freelance Editor

Some writers offered a wealth of craft tips and editing information on their early blogs. I know of several who were asked for beta reading help and then decided to hang out their shingles as editors.

Several of my old blogger friends are doing very well with these businesses. Their blogs gave them the cred they needed to establish themselves as professionals and provided a ready-made client list.

Book Cover Designer

A number of writer-bloggers I know had artistic backgrounds, so when they decided to join the indie publishing revolution, they designed their own covers.

Then they found that they could make good money designing covers for other indie authors. Most are still writing, but their cover design businesses allowed them to quit the day job.

Designer-Formatter

A lot of indies don't have the skills to format their own e-books or POD files (I sure don't.) Some tech-savvy authors found that formatting books paid more than writing them. They now have thriving formatting businesses.

Expert Speaker

Some author-bloggers discover they like this nonfiction-writing thing. Even though they started out writing fiction, writing nonfiction for a blog every week brought out their nonfiction talents.

They got into the short, informal essay format that the Web craves.

So they put the novels aside to write nonfiction books, articles, and web content on the subjects addressed in their blogs.

Slowly they became established experts. Now not only are they selling lots of nonfiction books, but they're in demand as public speakers who command big fees.

Publisher

Several of my early blogging friends are now publishers in their own right. They may have started a publishing business to publish their own books and then branched out and started soliciting submissions.

Others decided they'd seen too many great writers in their genre get stuck in the slush pile and decided to start a genre-specific small press.

Now they've got successful businesses.

Bestselling Self-Published Author

Many of my blog pals went the indie route while the rest of us were still on the query-go-round with agents.

Some went on to hit the *USA Today* and *New York Times* bestseller lists. Yes, it does happen.

Traditionally Published Author

I don't want to leave out the ones who did follow that path the rest of us were all trying to find. A bunch of my blog-friends got offers of representation from literary agents because of their blogs.

Note: This wasn't because they posted their WIPs and waited for an agent to show up with an offer of representation. That doesn't happen.

But they used their blogs for networking.

One was friendly with a blogger who became a literary agent. Another often visited a literary agent's blog and her query got noticed because the agent remembered her. Another had a publishing industry blog that agents often visited, so the agent knew her name.

Some of the most successful authors these days are the ones who started indie and got picked up by one of Amazon's imprints like Thomas and Mercer, Montlake, and Lake Union. Amazon imprints are sometimes listed as "indie" but they are really traditionally published, since Amazon pays advances (big ones) and royalties.

These authors used social media, including blogs, to create the kind of big platform that gets the attention of Amazon.

Not every writer needs to blog, but blogging can help your career in unexpected ways.

25—Should You Use a Pen Name?

A lot of beginning writers ask me if they should use a pen name for their blogs. They see all those business bloggers who call themselves "Foodie Gal" or "Techno-man" and figure they should do the same.

But this is another way that author blogs differ from business blogs. As I've said earlier, for an author, your name is your brand.

If you're an author who blogs, you want to blog with your author name, otherwise your work is wasted.

It's best to use your actual name if at all possible. These days when authors need to do their own marketing and "branding," simplifying the task is a good idea.

But Lots of Authors Write under Several Names!

Yes, but that's old school and unnecessary in most instances.

I know lots of popular authors have written under several names. Stephen King sometimes wrote as Richard Bachman (complete with a phony book jacket photo reputed to be his agent's insurance agent.); romance goddess Nora Roberts writes thrillers as J.D. Robb, and many authors use pen names when they write in different genres.

Traditional Reasons for Writing under a Pseudonym.

1) You write too fast for traditional publishing and you're only allowed one book a year under your current contract.

2) You want your readers to know exactly what to expect

from your brand (s).

3) Your writing might adversely affect your day job. (You're a youth minister who writes hard-core erotica.)

4) Your sales didn't live up to your publisher's sales expectations. (You've been told you'll never write in this town again.)

5) You have family issues (You're telling the thinly disguised story of your Uncle Charlie's secret life as a cabaret singer named Chardonnay.)

6) Your real name is Stephen King.

7) You think this book isn't "good enough" for your brand.

8) You're writing work-for-hire in a branded series (like all those writers who wrote Nancy Drew stories as "Caroline Keene.")

9) Your real name is too long for a book cover.

10) You have a snoozerific real name like John Smith or Anne Allen.

11) Your name is unpronounceable to most people who read in the language you write in.

Several of these are excellent arguments for writing under a name other than your own, but not for using *multiple* pen names.

Reasons #1, #4, and #8 only affect authors who are bound by old-school publishing contracts. These days, if you want to write faster than your contract stipulates, you can simply self-publish books in between releases. You can build on the brand name that you established as a traditionally-published author instead of going back to square one with a new name.

And although I see it a lot, I don't get #7. Going to all the trouble of building a separate brand for a book you aren't proud of makes no sense to me. If the book isn't working, get an editor or collaborator, or put the thing in a drawer and mine it for characters and short stories. I have at least a half dozen books that I don't want to put my name on, but I'm not going to inflict them on readers, under any name.

I do understand reason #2: You want to let readers know exactly what to expect when they pick up a book with that name on it.

But you can show genre in other ways, like cover design. And you can put helpful text on there like, "Romantic Suspense by ..." or "A [Sleuth's Name Here] Mystery by..." in your metadata and cover text.

J. K. Rowling tried using a pen name to write her mysteries. They got okay reviews but didn't sell all that well. But when Robert Galbraith was "outed" as J. K. Rowling, *The Cuckoo's Calling* soared to the top of the bestseller list.

So which would you rather have? A few not very observant readers who are disappointed that your mystery isn't one of your children's fantasy books...or millions of sales?

Other successful contemporary authors are luring their readers to cross those boundaries, too. Neil Gaiman writes everything from social satire to MG fantasy — and penned the screen adaptation of *Beowulf*-all under his own name. Rita Mae Brown writes literary LGBTQ+ novels, cat cozies, and historical Southern comedies all under her real name.

Writing in Many Genres Under One Name is Not a New Idea.

Carl Sandburg wrote everything from poetry to historical biography to children's stories — all under the same name.

Isaac Asimov famously wrote in "every category in the Dewey decimal system."

And yet you don't hear about people who bought *Asimov's Guide to Shakespeare* because they thought it was a science fiction novel. But a lot of people bought his Shakespeare guide because they knew his work in science fiction.

One of my favorite genre-jumpers was Mary Stewart, who not only invented contemporary romantic suspense, but wrote some of the best high fantasy ever.

And it may be that the digital era is changing things back to the way they were in earlier days. J.K. Rowling's success with *The Casual Vacancy* and *The Cuckoo's Calling* seems to show that brand trumps genre in today's world

Position in a brick and mortar bookstore isn't the primary factor in selling books in the era of Amazon: name recognition is. Brand trumps genre in today's publishing world.

26—Why I Don't Recommend Monetizing an Author Blog

How come I'm telling you not to follow the business blog path? Is it impossible for an author to do both?

No. Nothing is impossible if you have enough energy and time. And it helps to have a super-helpful spouse, no kids, and full staff of servants.

But don't some authors also have successful business blogs where they sell courses and make lots of money?

Yes. A handful of them do. But here's the thing: most of them didn't start recently.

As blogging author Delilah S. Dawson said at a seminar in 2016:

"How do I build a platform and make money with my blog?" a woman asks.

"Build a time machine and go back to 2005 and start your blog then."

But I didn't know that in 2015 when I tried to monetize our blog.

We were getting popular enough that the blog was attractive to pirates. One day I couldn't get in to upload a new post. I'd been locked out and a hacker had stolen all our content and pasted it into a monetized blog in Brazil.

Luckily I got some tech help and broke back in and changed the password.

But I realized we'd reached the point where we needed

the security of a self-hosted blog. Unfortunately, hosting costs money. Since I'd never heard anybody say there was a difference between author blogging and business blogging, I thought I'd give the monetizing thing a shot.

That meant getting some affiliates (companies that pay you a commission if a customer clicks through your site to theirs) and selling some advertising.

That turned out to be as bad an idea as Ms. Dawson suggested.

What about Affiliate Marketing?

I advised authors against most affiliate monetizing in my book with Catherine Ryan Hyde, *How to be a Writer in the E-Age.* There I pointed out that the profits from affiliate advertising are usually only a couple of dollars a month, and often you can't choose the ads. If you're a writer, you're likely to get ads on your site for scammy vanity presses and bogus literary agencies. Not exactly good for your brand.

However, you can also arrange affiliate status with Amazon and get a few pennies when people click through an Amazon link on your blog. Most book review bloggers do this, and although the payment is tiny, it gets reviewers at least a small payment for their work. That seemed like a good idea back when we wrote *How to be a Writer.*

But in late 2016, Amazon changed its review policy and started discouraging affiliates from writing customer reviews because that appeared to be "paying for reviews." Hundreds of book bloggers saw all their Amazon reviews removed—just because they got a dollar or two a month as an Amazon affiliate.

This new wrinkle makes Amazon affiliation even less attractive to bloggers, which is why I no longer recommend it.

Author Blog vs. Business Blog—Learning the Hard Way.

No kind of affiliate marketing was going to cover the cost of our expensive move from Blogger to the self-hosted site. So selling paid ads seemed to be the answer.

However, when we approached advertisers, we discovered that even a high profile writing blog with a pretty big audience was too small time to compete with the big business bloggers.

I learned I had to triple the number of followers, record podcasts, videos, and blog every day. I had to come up with "blogging courses" that we could charge thousands of dollars for, as well as pounding out dozens of how-to ebooks.

Otherwise, advertisers wouldn't pay any attention to us.

This essentially meant giving up my fiction writing career as well as my family, friends, and health.

I tried to do it for nearly a year, while spending endless days trying to fix all the tech glitches that happened when we moved from one platform to another.

I ended up working as an unpaid (and laughably incompetent) tech every waking minute. I had to abandon my two WIPs and cancel all guest posts and promotions for my latest book. My book page became a garbled mess I couldn't fix. My sales fell off a cliff.

I got a bunch of stress-related illnesses and developed painful arthritis in my fingers.

It was my doctor who finally put the kibosh on it. He said I wouldn't last the year if I kept working at that pace.

And I never did get the blog polished enough to sell any advertising.

That's when I realized people needed to differentiate between author blogging and business blogging. All the blogging advice out there wasn't aimed at me — or any author.

I went back to writing my mystery series and blogging once a week.

I had to relearn the fact that the primary reason for authors to blog can't be to make money with ads. We blog to interact with our readers. It's the book sales that will pay the bills, not the blog itself.

Big, Money-Making Blogs aren't Good for Selling Fiction.

Author blogs need to be inviting, fun, and above all...make readers feel comfortable. Ideally, they form a community. Their purpose is to provide a place where readers feel welcome to get to know the authors, the books, and other readers.

They offer value TO the reader.

Monetized blogs—especially the big, flashy ones that provide "make big bux blogging" advice—are usually impersonal. They'll have clickbait headers. They give advice on how to manipulate readers and boost your traffic so you can get high numbers to attract advertisers. They are all about SEO, stats, and clicks.

They get value FROM the reader.

Pyramid-Scheme Blogging is Fading

I don't know if our blog would ever have made money even if I had been able to pack 72 hours' worth of work into every 24 hour day. But I think the truth is most of those "blogging rules" don't work anymore.

That's because the blogs that dole out "blogging rules" are often those pyramid schemes I talked about in Chapter #3 and #5. They are asking for a lot of money for blogging courses that tell you how to teach courses that make a lot of money from other wannabe-bloggers.

But as Delilah Dawson said above, you won't get much of a ROI (Return on Investment) on the money you're paying for those courses, since the whole get-rich-blogging-about-blogging thing went out with late-night discussions of the latest plot twist on *Lost*.

***

Can somebody who has more energy and tech-savvy than this old Boomer successfully monetize an author blog?

They might. It might even be fun, especially with a partner. I'm not telling anybody not to try, but I figured I should at least share my cautionary tale.

27—Your Blogging Legacy: What to do When A Blogger Dies

I've lost a number of blogger friends over the years. A few died suddenly, so they were unable to let readers know what was happening.

One blogger who was a particular friend simply stopped blogging, and nobody had any idea why he had disappeared. Finally a former student left a comment on his last post saying my friend had died of a very aggressive form of cancer several months before. His grieving family had no idea what to do, because they weren't tech-savvy and didn't know how to access his blog or other social media accounts.

Without passwords and usernames to log in, heirs face a host of problems.

And any untended blog will attract endless spam invitations to meet hot women, buy fake college papers, and enlarge your penis. It also may attract the vicious trolls who love to taunt the bereaved with obscene messages on social media.

You really don't want this to be how people remember you. Yes, I know younger people don't think this applies to them. I was a firm believer in my own immortality until I was at least forty. But even young, healthy people get in accidents or are struck by sudden illnesses.

Not a nice thought, but it happens. Consider author-blogger Mac Tonnies, who updated his blog one night in 2009, went to bed and died of cardiac arrhythmia. He was 34. His blog, Posthuman Blues, is still just as he left it.

The thread of comments is heartbreaking — first expressions of annoyance from his regular followers about his lack of updates, then rumors, then the death announcement, then poignant memorials, then...spam.

One friend posted a comment in August of 2014, letting people know the blog had been turned into a book. And every so often a friend leaves a comment about how Mac is missed. But mostly the blog just collects those ads for Mumbai real estate and fake Viagra.

Without Mac's password, nobody can delete it or even disable the comments, and his digital remains may hang in limbo as long as there is an Internet.

The Web is crowded with ghosts like Mac Tonnies.

In fact, all of social media is crammed with dead people. Facebook is reported to lose 8000 people a day.

So now is the time to act if you don't want your cyber-remains to haunt the Web forever.

I suggest you appoint a social media executor right away. This doesn't have to be an official "digital executor," just somebody who's tech savvy that you trust with your personal information. You can appoint one informally without going through a lawyer.

All you need to do is make a "Password Passbook" for your executor. (But don't label it "password" because that's what hackers look for.) It's best to make hard copies too. Put this in a safe place with your other important documents and keep it updated regularly.

But you really do need one. A social media executor should:

• Close down or memorialize your social media accounts and notify online groups of your death. (Facebook has a mechanism for appointing an executor right on the site: go to your "Settings" page; choose "Security" and "Legacy Contact.")

- Maintain your blog as a memorial or delete it.

Plenty of blogs remain up long after the blogger has stopped updating them. They still can still be useful as long as comments are disabled and they're well maintained. Friends of the departed (fictional) Miss Snark have sustained her blog for agent-seekers in the "Snarkives" for over ten years.

28—Some Final Tips for Creating a Successful Author Blog

I've made some howling mistakes in my blogging career. The worst was trying to turn the blog into a business blog before I realized an author blog has a different purpose and goals.

Here are some things I learned from that failed experiment:

Define Success in Your Own Terms.

What defines success for one author may not satisfy another.

Checking your stats is fun for monitoring your progress, but those numbers mean very little for an author blog.

Superstar author Catherine Ryan Hyde sells tens of thousands of books a week, but her blog has a mediocre Alexa rating of nearly 3 million. My blog has an excellent Alexa rating of around 260 thousand. (It's like golf: the lower the number, the better.)

Do I sell tens of thousands of books a week? Um, er, not this week, anyway.

Stats and Alexa ratings are important to advertisers, but you're not advertising anything but yourself, so it's all good.

A small group of engaged readers can be much better for sales than a whole bunch of drive-bys. I recently visited a fellow author whose blog doesn't even rate an Alexa rank. But she gave me a rave review and I sold nearly 40 books within hours.

My launch on my own blog the next day made fewer sales.

Who has the more successful blog for a fiction writer? Obviously she does.

Keep up Your Brand.

Ruth and I have spent years on our blog building a reputation for being friendly, savvy, and straightforward. We both write upmarket fiction about classy women. That's our brand.

The "blogging rules" for business blogs and online marketing often tell you to act sleazy and bully people with popups and other nasty tech tricks. Serious disconnect there. No amount of SEO will make up for alienating your core readership.

Be Generous.

Owners of monetized and business blogs often worry that other bloggers will steal their content. But we authors want you to "steal" our content and spread it all over the Web. (Just link back to the blog and spell our names right.)

However, when I told our expensive web host I wanted protection from hackers, they put some awful thing on the blog that made it impossible to copy the content and post it to other blogs. I got called on the carpet for this by some of the biggest names in the industry and I had no idea it had happened or how to stop it. (I finally did get word to the right people and that "protection" went away.)

But I ended up looking like a paranoid doofus.

Don't Use Gimmicks to Build Traffic.

Learning how to manipulate Google can be very handy and can help you get a higher ranking in search engines. But when you're starting out, your traffic is more likely to come from networking and social media. A new blog will get most of its traffic from posts and shares on social media or other blogs, not Google searches.

People will subscribe and come back if you are engaging and fun. It's much more important to be friendly and have something interesting to offer than it is to have the right keywords, post frequency, or word count.

Networking with other bloggers will probably be your number one source of traffic when you're starting out. That means making friends, not tricking people.

Content is Still King.

Some techies may have to game the system to get readers, but that's because they don't have the writer's skill set. For a writer, good writing is more important than SEO.

A friend once told me about an impressive guy who was going to dominate the book world because he was a major expert in SEO and had bought up a whole lot of book related domain names. So I went to Impressive Guy's website, which had the great domain name like books dot com.

But there was nothing on the site but about 300 clunky, repetitive words about how to choose a good book. It boiled down to: read the *New York Times Book Review*.

In other words, the site was worthless. Nobody was going to visit it twice. Manipulating the algorithms may get short-term results, but it's not helpful in the long run.

Good writers don't need gimmicks. We only need to entertain and inform: content really is king. Be accessible and be yourself. Nothing else matters. (Well, correct spelling and grammar do help.)

Don't Relinquish Control of Your Blog.

Unglamorous low tech is better than tech-heavy stuff you can't do yourself. Your blog is the face you show to the world. You'll be held responsible for whatever happens there.

I should have taken at least three months to learn to use WordPress dot org before we moved from Blogger, but I let fear and tech experts talk me out of my comfort zone.

My expert help almost immediately became unavailable due to a family tragedy. And I almost ended up as a tragedy myself.

None of that would have happened if I'd insisted on keeping more control.

Don't Sacrifice Your WIP for Your Blog.

I listened to business blog gurus who called me a slacker because I didn't want to spend eighteen hours a day blogging. Publishers' deadlines meant nothing to them. Nothing mattered but blog stats and subscriber numbers.

When it was finally over, I realized all the advice I was getting was irrelevant to my needs and just plain wrong for an author.

Make Your Goal Networking, not Sales.

The sales will come. The more friends and contacts you have, the more sales in the long run. But treating a friend as a sales target will backfire.

Ask for Help when You Need It.

A number of readers offered to help me early on during the disastrous monetizing experiment, but I was afraid to admit defeat.

Our blog only exists because of the wonderful people who stepped up and made the offer again. We are now at a new self-hosted WordPress dot org site, with a simpler template, and we are not monetized. Our generous host is Bakerview Consulting. I will forever be grateful to tech-wizard Barb Drozdowich, the owner of Bakerview. Barb believes authors shouldn't monetize, and now I realize she's right.

Remember the Best Marketing Rule is the Golden One.

It's worth saying it one more time. Almost everything in contemporary Internet sales and marketing is based on a false premise: a marketer's job is to bully and trick customers, not give them what they want.

But the most successful online retailer, Amazon, doesn't use this method. Instead their goal is customer satisfaction.

You'll have a much more successful blog — and writing career — if you put the customer first and ignore all the other "rules" of marketing.

***

Blogging isn't for everybody. But it can be a fantastic marketing tool for authors who are willing to put in the time. So ignore most of what you've read about blogging and start an easy, friendly, low-stress author blog.

In the long run, a relaxed author blog will sell your books better than all the aggressive, money-making blogging tactics in the world. Plus it cuts way down on your advertising expenses.

An author blog will give you a secure place to interact with your fans and draw new readers. And for a lot of us, it's just plain fun.

Happy blogging!

A Note from Anne

This book is not intended to be a comprehensive manual for bloggers. There are already some great books out there for author-bloggers that go into much more technical detail.

Here are some I recommend:

Blogging for Writers: How Authors & Writers Build Successful Blogs (2014)
by Robin Houghton
This is a beautifully illustrated print book from Writer's Digest Books. Its illustrations walk you through a lot of the technical aspects of blogging.

Blogging for Authors (2016)
By Barb Drozdowich
This one is also nicely illustrated and it's available in both print and ebook. Barb is a tech and media consultant and an expert in WordPress.

Blog it! The Author's Guide to Building a Successful Online Brand (2013)
By Molly Greene
A complete manual for using your blog to build your brand. Molly is a mystery author and popular blogger with a fun, humorous style.

Blogging Just for Writers (2013)
By Frances Caballo
Frances is a social media strategist and the social media manager for the San Francisco Writer's Conference. No-nonsense guidance for writer-bloggers.

Rise of the Machines: Human Authors in a Digital World (2013)
By Kristen Lamb
Social Media ninja and uber-blogger Kristen Lamb is irreverent and outspoken—and she knows her stuff. This is a great guide to establishing an online presence and making new technology your friend.

SMART Book Marketing For Authors Power Pack (2017)
By Chris Syme
Chris is a social media marketing consultant who has a fantastic weekly podcast on book marketing. These three books help authors use social media efficiently without letting it swallow up all your writing time.

About the Author

Anne R. Allen is a popular blogger and the author of the hilarious Camilla Randall Mysteries as well as the comic novels *Food of Love, The Gatsby Game,* and *The Lady of the Lakewood Diner.* She's also the co-author, with Catherine Ryan Hyde, of the writer's guide HOW TO BE A WRITER IN THE E-AGE.

Anne is a graduate of Bryn Mawr College and now lives on the Central Coast of California near San Luis Obispo, the town Oprah called "the happiest town in America."

Anne has a blog for Camilla fans at Anne R. Allen's Books She loves to hear from her readers! Contact her at annerallen.allen@gmail.com

Anne R. Allen's Blog...with Ruth Harris, was named one of the Best 101 Websites for Writers by *Writer's Digest.* Visit her there, or on Twitter, Facebook, Goodreads, Pinterest, **or** LinkedIn.

If you've enjoyed this book, we hope you will consider writing a brief review. It will help others find the book. Thanks!

Books by Anne R. Allen

THE CAMILLA RANDALL MYSTERIES: Chick Lit Noir— Snarky, delicious fun! These books are a laugh-out-loud mashup of romantic comedy, crime fiction, and satire. Think Bridget Jones meets Miss Marple. The first three Camilla books are available in a convenient boxed set.

#1 GHOSTWRITERS IN THE SKY: After her celebrity ex-husband's ironic joke about her "kinky sex habits" is misquoted in a tabloid, New York etiquette columnist Camilla Randall's life unravels in bad late night TV jokes. Nearly broke and down to her last Hermes scarf, she accepts an invitation to a Z-list Writers' Conference in the wine-and-cowboy town of Santa Ynez, California, where, unfortunately, a cross-dressing dominatrix named Marva plies her trade by impersonating Camilla. When a ghostwriter's plot to blackmail celebrities with faked evidence leads to murder, Camilla must team up with Marva to stop the killer from striking again.

#2 SHERWOOD, LTD: Suddenly-homeless American manners expert Camilla Randall becomes a 21st century Maid Marian—living rough near the real Sherwood Forest with a band of outlaw English erotica publishers—led by a charming, self-styled Robin Hood who unfortunately may intend to kill her.

#3 THE BEST REVENGE (the prequel): Read how it all began. In the glitzy 1980s, a teenaged Camilla loses everything: fortune, love, and eventually even her freedom when a TV star's murder is mistakenly laid at her feet. Through it all, she perseveres, and comes to learn that she is made of sterner stuff than anyone might have imagined, herself included.

#4 NO PLACE LIKE HOME: Doria Windsor, the uber-rich editor of *Home* decorating magazine loses everything, including her Ponzi-schemer husband, when their luxury wine-country home mysteriously goes up in flames. Homeless, destitute, presumed dead and branded a criminal, 59-yr-old Doria has a crash course in reality…and a second chance at love.

Meanwhile, Camilla Randall is facing homelessness, too, as Doria's husband's schemes unravel and take down innocent bystanders along the way. When the mysterious — and dangerously attractive — Mr. X. turns up at Camilla's bookstore looking for clues to the death of a missing homeless man, Camilla joins in the search.

With the help of brave trio of homeless people and a little dog named Toto, Doria, Camilla and Mr. X journey down their own yellow brick road to unmask the real killer and reveal the dark secrets of Doria's "financial wizard" husband.

#5 SO MUCH FOR BUCKINGHAM: Camilla makes the mistake of responding to an Amazon review of one of her etiquette guides and sets off a chain of events that leads to arson, attempted rape and murder. Her best friend Plantagenet Smith is accused of the murder and nobody but her shady former boyfriend Peter Sherwood — fresh from a Tasmanian prison — can save him.

Camilla and Plant are caught between rival factions of historical reenactors who are fiercely pro or anti-Richard III. Set against the backdrop of Richard's re-burial in Leicester in 2015, the book is an exploration of the power of false rumors as well as a satire of the Internet communities whose "flame wars" sometimes spill into real life.

***

FOOD OF LOVE (Romantic-comedy/thriller)   After Princess Regina, a former supermodel, is ridiculed in the tabloids for gaining weight, someone tries to kill her. She suspects her royal husband wants to be rid of her, now she's no longer model-thin. As she flees the mysterious assassin, she discovers the world thinks she is dead, and seeks refuge with the only person she can trust: her long-estranged foster sister, Rev. Cady Stanton, a right-wing talk show host who has romantic and weight issues of her own. Cady delves into Regina's past and discovers Regina's long-lost love, as well as dark secrets that connect them all.

THE GATSBY GAME (Romantic-comedy /
mystery): When Fitzgerald-quoting con man Alistair Milborne is found dead a movie star's motel room — igniting a world-wide scandal — the small-town police can't decide if it's an accident, suicide, or foul play. As evidence of murder emerges, Nicky Conway, the smart-mouth nanny, becomes the prime suspect. She's the only one who knows what happened. But she also knows nobody will ever believe her. The story is based on the real mystery surrounding the death of David Whiting, actress Sarah Miles' business manager, during the filming of the 1973 Burt Reynolds movie *The Man Who Loved Cat Dancing*.

THE LADY OF THE LAKEWOOD DINER (Literary comedy/mystery) Someone has shot aging bad-girl rocker Morgan le Fay and threatens to finish the job. Is it fans of her legendary dead rock-god husband, Merlin? Or is the secret buried in her childhood hometown of Avalon, Maine? Morgan's childhood best friend Dodie, the no-nonsense owner of a dilapidated diner, may be the only one who knows the dark secret that can save Morgan's life. And both women may find that love really is better the second time around. Echoes of the Grail legend bring into focus the nature of nostalgia and the pitfalls of longing for a Golden Age that never was.

These three comic novels are available in a boxed set called **BOOMER WOMEN: THREE COMEDIES ABOUT A GENERATION THAT CHANGED THE WORLD**

WHY GRANDMA BOUGHT THAT CAR: A collection of short stories and verses—humorous portraits of rebellious women at various stages of their lives. From aging Betty Jo, who feels so invisible she contemplates robbing a bank, to neglected 10-year-old Maude, who turns to a fantasy Elvis for the love she's denied by her patrician family, to a bloodthirsty Valley Girl version of Madam Defarge, these women—young and old—are all rebelling against the stereotypes and traditional roles that hold them back. Which is, of course, why Grandma bought that car...

Other Nonfiction by Anne R. Allen

HOW TO BE A WRITER IN THE E-AGE: A SELF-HELP GUIDE co-written with Amazon superstar Catherine Ryan Hyde. This guide offers warm, friendly advice on how to start and sustain a writing career. You'll see a lot of books out there about how to write, and a whole lot more that promise ebook millions. But this book is different. It helps you establish a professional writing career in this time of rapid change — and answers the questions so many writers are asking: Does an author still need an agent? Can new writers still get published by Big Five publishers? What about digital-only imprints, mid-sized publishers, small presses — or should everybody self-publish? Do you need to spend endless hours on social media? How do you cope with rejection, depression, bad reviews and other downsides of the writing profession? Anne and Catherine answer all these questions and more in this fun, information-packed book.